Laurel,

My prayer and hope is that
you continue to find yourself
on this journey of life and that
your soul can have hope.

Love,
Karen R. Hobbs

UNLOCKING
MY SOUL TO
HOPE AGAIN

Hope and Healing from Childhood Sexual Abuse

KAREN R. HOBBS

Exulon
ELITE

www.xulonpress.com

Endorsements:

Karen's powerful and compelling story shows how God has walked alongside her and comforted her throughout all the stages of her pain, as He is willing to do for all sexual abuse survivors. This small book will help give the "big people" in a child's life the ability to spot the disaster before it happens. It will also give them the ability to see the symptoms of on-going sexual abuse so they can intervene and interrupt it, and to help them to walk alongside the adult survivor of Childhood Sexual abuse knowing that the survivor's pain will go through many different healing stages but can never be erased.

> Michael Sharman, J.D. "Attorney committed to fighting for justice and healing for victims of Childhood Sexual Abuse."

Karen is the remarkable example of the maturity that results from determined struggle against formidable difficulties. I have known Karen for the past twenty-five years. What is unique about Karen is not the severe abuse she endured, but her remarkable response. One definition for courage is facing our fears and choosing to take action. She lives out Galatians (NIV) 6:9, "Let us not become weary in doing good for at the proper time we will reap a harvest if we do not give up." Karen's reward was not only to finally see that her abuser was removed from the possibility of abusing other children but also the character she developed in overcoming her abuse and her ability to help others through her knowledge and compassion.

> Richard A. Betts, Lt. Col Retired, USAF, Licensed Professional Counselor, Certified Substance Abuse Counselor

"I have known Karen professionally and personally for many years, and I continue to be impressed and encouraged by her journey of overcoming years of abuse. Her faith in God, her tenacity and courage serve as a powerful witness for those who find themselves on a similar path. I know that her openness about her own struggles and triumph that she shares in this book will provide a catalyst of hope for hurting souls. I thank God for her."

Dr J. Douglas Duty Jr.
Senior Pastor
Turner Memorial Baptist Church

Dedication

To my children, for giving me the motivation to find my voice so that I could unlock my soul to hope again. Also to my Heavenly Father for being my strength and refuge during my most difficult and painful times.

Acknowledgements

Thank you to my family who loved me through the difficult times and who are always willing to celebrate the small victories with me.

Thank you to my pastor, who was willing to step into a place of uncertainty with me, so I could learn how to trust and obey God's still small voice, in order to transform my fear of God into a deep longing and desire to know the depth of His love for me. What a truly magnificent spiritual transformation that has been.

To my therapists, who walk beside me into some very dark and painful places. Their willingness to engage on this journey without judgment and condemnation has helped me to be known by them as well as by myself.

To the legal team who worked on my behalf to help me engage my voice in order for me to tell my story and to find justice this side of heaven. Your compassion, commitment, and support never did and never will go unnoticed. Thank you for your willingness to fight on behalf of those who have been hurt so deeply that they no longer feel like they have a voice.

To my friends and fellow alumni, thank you for the love, support, and words of encouragement as I closed a difficult and painful chapter of my life. My prayer is God will use these words to bring some healing to those who were not able to speak the truth of their own pain.

To my clients, for being the catalyst for me to continue to work towards greater healing personally so that professionally I can grow to be the tool through which God can work to bring healing to others.

To the staff at Xulon Publishing, for being willing to take on this project and to put words to my story. This book would not be possible without your support and expertise.

Finally, to God my Father, who has given the desire to tell my story for the purpose of allowing myself and others to see how He works in our moments of pain, and how my story aligns with His story of amazing and redemptive grace. To God be the glory!

Table of Contents

Preface

Adult Survivor of Childhood Sexual Abuse

*M*y name is Karen Hobbs and I am an Adult Survivor of Childhood Sexual Abuse as well as a licensed therapist in Virginia. I am looking for resources and was wondering if your office had any recommendations. June of 2013, I went to police in regards to my childhood abuse. I was abused by an ordained pastor and teacher at the Christian school I attended. For five years, day in and day out I was molested and raped. When the school was notified, they fired the teacher and said it was an inappropriate consensual relationship with a student. Nothing else was done. He was forty-seven at the time the abuse began and I was twelve.

When I went to the police, I was wired and I made a call to the offender. He confessed to what he had done on the call to me and later in an interview with the police. To this day, he still does not believe he has done anything wrong. Last Monday, he pled guilty to forcible sodomy and was taken to jail for what will probably be the rest of his life. I am reaching out to you to see if you are aware of or if the doctor has any resources on what happens after the court process. The crime *was twenty-seven years ago. Justice has been served and you would think that would be the end. However, I am finding that I am struggling, just in a different way. Emotionally I am all over the place. I have an amazing Christian psychiatrist who also does therapy with me so I have the support. I am just wondering if there is something you are aware of that would help me understand what is going on. Thank you in advance for your time and assistance with this matter.*

Sincerely,
Karen R. Hobbs

I received this response from Dr. Dodd

Dear Karen,

Sadly, I have no data or information to offer in part because few people have had the courage to do what you have done. Those who have had the courage often see the courts dismiss these cases for lack of corroborating testimony. I am grateful beyond words, he will spend the rest of his dark life behind bars. Now that some form of human justice has been meted out, there is the task of coming to terms that vindication is neither sweet nor satisfying, but it is right. There is goodness and honor in allowing what satisfaction that is available to be taken in.

In one sense, the working toward an end, a completion like this exposes the reality that any completion on this earth is only a small taste of what we really want. It is the paradox that we work for years to achieve a goal, and then when it is finished, it is more haunting and disruptive than we could have predicted. I have seen this in so many endeavors. Writing a book or finishing a dissertation is haunting because after all the work, the "achievement" can't compensate for the work that was required to arrive at the goal. In fact, there is almost a sense of mockery: All this work, for what?

When the goal is not the achievement of a task but the pursuit of justice, it is even harder. Justice is truly only finished by the perpetrator standing before the face of God. What your heart wants is for that man to confess with grief and humility his profound, utterly profound crimes against your body and heart. To think the school said he was involved in inappropriate consensual activity is ludicrous. It is worse than ludicrous. It is criminal, ungodly, if not outright evil. I am incensed. But that is the ripple effect of this evil perpetrated against you. There are so many who need to be indicted and held accountable and it will not come until the day of the Lord.

What do I recommend? Honor the small droplets of justice. Know that it is actually more haunting and heartbreaking than satisfying, but what satisfaction can be held and tasted and allowed to be a foretaste of what is to come: may it be blessed. I am grateful beyond words that you are working with a man of radical goodness, wisdom, and depth.

Blessings to you and may your story and your life be a gift to so, so many. –Dr. Dodd

Introduction

Prayer from a Young Wounded Heart

You have searched me, LORD,
and you know me.
You know when I sit and when I rise;
you perceive my thoughts from afar.
You discern my going out and my lying down;
you are familiar with all my ways.
Before a word is on my tongue
you, LORD, know it completely.
You hem me in behind and before,
and you lay your hand upon me.
Such knowledge is too wonderful for me,
too lofty for me to attain.
Where can I go from your Spirit?
Where can I flee from your presence?
If I go up to the heavens, you are there;
if I make my bed in the depths, you are there.

If I rise on the wings of the dawn,
if I settle on the far side of the sea,
even there your hand will guide me,
your right hand will hold me fast.
If I say, "Surely the darkness will hide me
and the light become night around me,"
even the darkness will not be dark to you;
the night will shine like the day,
for darkness is as light to you.

For you created my inmost being;
you knit me together in my mother's womb.
I praise you because I am fearfully and wonderfully made;
your works are wonderful,
I know that full well.
My frame was not hidden from you
when I was made in the secret place,
when I was woven together in the depths of the earth.
Your eyes saw my unformed body;
all the days ordained for me were written in your book
before one of them came to be.
(Psalm 139:1-16 NIV)

We read this passage of scripture and realize how amazing it is that God formed us so uniquely. It even encourages us to receive comfort from the fact our heavenly Father knows everything about us. He knows where we are, what we are doing, and even knows what we are going to say before we say it. However, when something bad happens to us we begin to ask some very emotional questions.

I wrote this letter to my brother, Jesus, after suffering at the hands of men who were supposed to be trusted. I laid my wounded heart out before Jesus as I sought the answers to these heart rendering questions about our Father God.

Jesus,

I come to you because I am lonely and confused! I am hoping you can answer some questions about our Father. I often find myself in a very dark and lonely place. I am completely exposed and vulnerable, crying out to God to deliver me from the physical pain and suffering that tears through my body. In the midst of my tears there is nothing but complete silence! I look around and there is nothing!

Where is our Father – has He turned His back on me?
Does He just stand and watch as men seek
to violate and shame me?
Why doesn't He do something?
Can't He see the pain that I am in?
Doesn't He care?

*Psalm 139 says that God searches and knows me.
He knows when I sit and when I rise; He perceives
my thoughts from afar. He discerns my going out
and my lying down; He is familiar with all my
ways. Before a word is on my tongue He knows it
completely.*

**If He knew ahead of time what I was going
to ask of Him, why wasn't He ready to help?
What kept Him from intervening in the
moments of my darkest pain and shame?**

*Psalm 139 goes on to say that God created my
inmost being, He knit me together in my mother's
womb. I praise you because I am fearfully and wonderfully made; your works are wonderful, I know
that full well. My frame was not hidden from you
when I was made in the secret place. When I was
woven together in the depths of the earth your eyes
saw my unformed body. All the days ordained for
me were written in your book before one of them
came to be.*

**How could God create me knowing the intense pain
and loneliness I would encounter?
If He knew what laid ahead for me why did
He even allow my life to be?**

What kept Him from creating a different path for me?
Why was I chosen to endure so much shame and
humiliation from a very young age?
He is a Father, doesn't that mean He is supposed to love
and protect His children?
Where is He when I need Him most?
I don't understand?
What kind of life is this for a Father to choose for His child,
especially when I am created in His image?
What is the purpose?

If you are a victim of childhood sexual abuse, you may have asked some of these same questions. My prayer now is that as you read through my journey through survival to overcomer, it will help you become not only a survivor, but an overcomer as well.

If you are not a survivor but are in a position to either prevent abuse or to help past or present victims of sexual abuse, then my prayer is that this book will help you understand the structure of sexual abuse. As you read through this journey from survival to overcomer, you will see into the mind and soul of a sexual abuse survivor. May these words help you walk alongside a survivor knowing that the survivor's pain will go through different healing stages but can never be erased.

Chapter 1

From Innocence to Rape

Prior to June of 1982, I was a typical little girl. I enjoyed life, most of the time, and my biggest worry was when my mom and dad would be home from work. I was twelve years old and struggling through puberty, trying to figure out where I fit in this great big world. I was growing into my body and trying to make sense of all the crazy and irrational emotions and thoughts I was experiencing. I loved to talk, had friends that I loved spending time with, and was a very compliant and respectful little girl. I was "that girl" who developed early and who was taller than all the boys in her class. Yet, I was still a little girl who went home at night and would fall asleep with her teddy bear and dog snuggled up next to her.

I grew up in a home where my parents did the best they could with what they knew and I always knew that I was loved. It was a day and age where sex was not spoken of and was reserved for marriage. No one talked about "inappropriate touching" or "safe touch." Television was still airing family shows and was not bombarding society with shows full of sexually explicit material. My parents were committed to rearing my siblings and me in a Christian home and sacrificed financially to place us in a Christian school. Their desire was that a Christian school would provide a better education in a smaller, more caring environment. It would be in this environment where I would meet Smite and my life would change forever.

A Very Tumultuous Time

By June of 1982, I had just completed my seventh grade year of school. I'd had Smite for study hall that year (1981-1982). Throughout that school year, Smite would put his hands on my shoulder or touch me on the back, occasionally giving me a full body hug. At the time I thought nothing about it, but looking back it was rather odd and uncomfortable. Smite would also touch and hug other girls, so it did not occur to me that he was being inappropriate. In my eyes he was just an "old man," especially to a twelve-year old who was so consumed with her world and figuring life out. It was just not a big deal. However, he was "grooming me" for the next stage of his perverted plan.

Looking back, I now know that this was the beginning of what would become a very tumultuous time in my life.

22

June of 1982 became a very emotional time for me. In the midst of losing my best friend, I was also going through puberty, and my world seemed to be crashing down around me. This became Smite's opportunity to step in and "save the day." This was the next phase of abuse or as he likes to refer to it, "the affair." That June day in 1982, when he cornered me in the "book room" and I responded, "No," when he asked if I knew what French kissing was and offered to show me would become the moment that would forever change the course of my life.

The Sexual Abuse Begins

Eighth grade began in the fall of 1982. A couple of weeks into the start of school, Smite began singling me out. He would then begin French kissing me. His mouth always tasted like cinnamon Mentos because he was always chewing on those. While kissing me, he would fondle me. This would happen pretty much every day to some degree. Around the end of November, he started putting his hands in my pants. He also began to force me to engage in oral sex on him on a regular basis. When I would refuse, he forced me to do it. That always made me sick! Then he began engaging in the oral sex with me. He would get angry at me if I did not indicate to him I enjoyed what was happening. I never did enjoy it!

I learned early on to just zone out because that was easier to deal with than the reality of what was happening or to even fight it. These events, to a varying degree, happened on a daily basis throughout the next four years if we were both at school. He would also call my house in the mornings, let the phone ring once and then I was to call him back and listen to his perverted explanations of what he was doing while he masturbated on the other end of the phone. If I didn't call back once that phone rang, then whatever his plan for that day for me would be much harsher or more painful.

As we were getting close to the end of the school year, Smite began to get much more comfortable with molesting me. Oral sex was happening almost every day. One morning he picked me up early for school, and when we got to the building there were not many people there. He took me up to the K4 room where he proceeded to kiss me and fondle me which moved into oral sex. He held me down on the table and decided to move us to the next step, though he did not go "all the way." It was, however, incredibly painful!

When he was done, he told me to get dressed, go downstairs to the bathroom, and wash with warm, soapy water. I washed and cried, then went through the rest of the day hurting and numb trying to pretend like nothing happened. He continued to look at me or kiss me or fondle me if he got an opportunity. He always would say to me after he did something, "Thanks for making my day!"

I was truly looking forward to summer break so I would not have to deal with the daily stress caused by Smite's abuse. I babysat in my old neighborhood during this summer, so I wasn't even at my home. I thought this would keep him away from me all summer, however, he soon learned where I was and would come over to the townhouse. The children I watched were two and nine months old. For about a two or three-week span, he would show up at the house and try to get me to engage in some form of oral sex with him. Fortunately, he eventually stopped coming to the house and I was able to finish the summer without contact with him.

Raped

The following year started out being just more of the same old stuff as the previous school year. However, in late October my grandfather got very sick and my parents were going back and forth to Alabama on a pretty regular basis. During this time, there was a morning which Smite gave me a ride to school, though I had been avoiding allowing him to pick me up. We got to the school at about 7:30 A.M. and Smite took me to an upstairs room of the school. He began kissing me and pulling me to him, however, I pushed him away. I didn't want him touching me. I didn't want him near me. I had made up my mind I was not going to be part of his fantasy any longer.

However, the more I pushed him away the tighter he grabbed me. At some point, he pushed me back on a desk and forcefully raped me. I tried to pull away, but realized that the more I fought the more painful it became. From that point on I quit fighting. I just dissociated. He then told me if I told anyone what happened, I would never see my family or anyone else I knew ever again. Fear now entered the equation.

For the next three school years, I would encounter daily episodes of some type of sexual assault. It could range from a simple kiss on the cheek to full-fledged rape and everything in between. Sometimes it would be during class, sometimes outside of class, sometimes at school, and sometimes at home. There was never a moment of peace or a place of refuge! I was always looking, always wondering, always on guard to what would happen next. Even summer vacation wasn't a time of refuge or peace.

September of 1984, school once again started back up, but the new thing this year was I was in his classroom on a more frequent basis. We were given assigned seats and my seat was at his desk either right next to him or across from him. When sitting next to him I would have to concentrate on class assignments while he proceeded to try to find ways to fondle me. I was horrified and humiliated, praying none of my peers would see what he was doing. This happened every day during that class period for that entire year and the following year as well.

In October of 1984, I also made public my profession of faith. When I was seven years old I accepted Jesus as my personal Lord and Savior. It wasn't until October of 1984 at the age of fourteen that I made that profession public and was baptized. The day of my baptism was huge for me. My siblings and I entered the baptismal and were all baptized at the same time. That Sunday evening, I went home and I felt truly "clean." I felt for the first time in a long time that God looked favorably upon me and did not see me as broken and damaged. That did not last even 24 hours, as the next day in school I would be violated all over again by Smite. Once again I felt damaged and broken and disgusting in the sight of God.

For the five years that the sexual abuse was going on, I would find myself waking in the middle of the night terrified and crying. I would be awakened by a nightmare or by a sudden noise that made me think that Smite had come into my room. Sometimes I would experience body memories, where it felt like Smite was actually touching me, or kissing me, or raping me. I would try to push him away but it did not stop! That occurred on the nights I could sleep.

Other nights I would lie awake wondering what I would encounter the next day. Over and over again those thoughts and visions played out in my head. I would get nauseated, sometimes vomit, and I would have excruciating cramps to the point that even walking was extremely painful. Each day I had to muster up the strength to go to school and face whatever lay ahead, just hoping and praying I would survive one more day. A good day was when I came home not bleeding. A bad day was coming home wondering how to get the bleeding to stop or if it would stop! Those latter days were more frequent than I cared to count.

While the actual sexual assaults were happening, I found myself completely disconnected from self. I became an observer of the abuse rather than an active participant. In the counseling world this phenomenon is called dissociation. I would emotionally disconnect from my physical body and I would take my position in the corner of the room and just watch as Smite would kiss, fondle, molest, or rape "some young girl." In my mind it wasn't me. It couldn't be me. To acknowledge it was me would result in my inability to walk out of that room or to even survive. So, I waited until he was done, then I would put the girl back together, and "we" would carry on until the next time. For five years there was always a next time. Sometimes it would be later that day, or the next school day, or the next time he just showed up at my house, or he just "stopped by" while I was working.

My Best Friend Returns

During the school years of 85-86 and 86-87, my best friend and her family returned from Germany. Once she was back, we picked up right where we had left off three years earlier, though I knew I could not tell her what had been happening to me. We became inseparable and though she didn't realize it, she became a life-saver for me. Where you saw one of us you saw us both. I felt somewhat safe now because it became harder for Smite to get me alone. He would on occasion be able to create an opportunity to get me alone and engage in the same behavior as the previous years. However, to my relief, it was not as likely to be a daily occurrence now that my best friend was back.

Late in September, the opportunity presented itself in which he had to take me home after school. When we got to my house, I jumped out of the car and went quickly up to the door to unlock it and go in. When I went to shut the door, however, he was right behind me. He stuck his foot in the door before I could close it and forced his way in. I dropped my stuff on the sofa right in front of the door and told him he couldn't be here.

Though I tried to stand up for myself, he grabbed me and forcefully began kissing me. He then took me by the arm and pulled me into my parents' bedroom right around the corner from the family room. There he pushed me onto the bed and pulled his pants off. I pulled back on the bed, but he grabbed me, held me tightly, and forced himself on me. He pulled out before ejaculating, pulled his pants up, got some toilet paper and threw it at me, then left the house thanking me once again for "making his day!" I took a shower and discovered I had bruising on my thighs from his rough forceful treatment. I sat on the bed and cried!

Later that night, he and his wife came by the house to "check" on my brother, sister, and I because my parents were out of town and a young teacher from the school was staying with us. I think he just came by to intimidate me and to scare me into being quiet. It was just one more way of reminding me that I could not get away from him.

During November and December of 1985, when my friend wasn't with me, I did everything I could to avoid contact with Smite. One day after school, he found me hiding out in the basement of the school. He angrily grabbed me up from out of the corner. I started crying and asked him to leave me alone. He put something up against my neck and told me he would hurt me if I didn't be quiet. I immediately dissociated as he forced me into oral then full sex. I went to the bathroom and cleaned up, again crying. There was a red mark where something had been pressed into my neck.

As the 1985-86 school year was quickly approaching the end, I suddenly found myself alone in Smite's room. He was beginning to fondle me and preparing for oral sex when he heard someone coming. He pushed me into a room right off his classroom and told me to get dressed and be quiet. I then heard him talking to two other students. About twenty minutes later he opened the door and let me out. I took off as fast as I could and never looked back.

My senior year was much less eventful than the previous years had been. There was the occasional kiss or fondling, sometimes over clothes, sometimes skin to skin contact. There really wasn't much intercourse that happened that I can recall at this time. By this time, it was winding down for whatever reason to which I was extremely grateful. However, I believe the reason it was winding down was because Dory had returned from Germany the prior year and we became inseparable!

How could God, my teachers, and the other adults in my life not see what was happening to me? I decided I would make them pay by speaking my mind, doing what I felt was in my best interest, and standing up to the hypocrisy that surrounded me! I had reached a breaking point! I was no longer a helpless little twelve-year-old girl though I was still afraid to disclose what had been happening to me!

By this point in my life, I had also become angry at everyone around me.

Finally, in June of 1987, I graduated from high school and felt as if I had been paroled from a sentence of shame, pain, and torment. I thought I could finally put this behind me. I was free at last, or so I thought!

From innocence to rape was a tough chapter of my life to relive, but I pray that if you were a victim of childhood sexual abuse, my sharing it will encourage you to tell someone about what has happened to you.

> ➤ Find someone you trust and share what happened to you.
> ➤ Get professional counseling to help you deal with what has been done to you.
> ➤ You may think you can suppress it and disassociate, but as you will see in the next chapter, it will eventually impact every area of your life.
> ➤ For those of you who live or work with survivors of sexual abuse can you sense, imagine, and feel what the victim may have felt during the abuse.

Chapter 2

Dealing with the After Shock

It was not until I began college that I was able to put words to what had happened to me during high school. When I began my course of study in psychology, on my road to becoming a licensed counselor, I realized that what I encountered during the course of my education at the Christian school was sexual abuse and rape. I would encounter many, many years of intense flashbacks of abuse and rape, several attempts to kill myself, an intense desire to die, and many, many years of feeling the shame and guilt of not standing up to Smite. The shame, the spiritual damage, the hate and disdain towards myself have been huge obstacles for me to overcome as I tried to get to this place where I could tell my story. My prayer is it will help others to be able to tell their story and experience God's amazing grace and healing to the extent to which it can be experienced on this side of heaven.

Impact on Relationships

The sexual abuse at the hands of Smite has impacted almost every area of my life. In my marriage I quite frequently find myself where intimate contact or touch triggers a flashback. The result is I push my husband away or I become a spectator instead of an active participant in the sexual relationship with my husband. More often than not, I dissociate during intercourse and once it is done, I curl up into a fetal position and cry myself to sleep. The loneliness and abandonment I feel during this time is so intense I want to crawl into a hole and die.

This creates quite a struggle in my marriage and is not a burden my husband should have to carry.

My pregnancies were also quite challenging as there were ample times in which I was triggered into a flashback. Every time I had a prenatal check-up, I had to be talked through the procedure in an attempt to keep me from being triggered into a full-fledged panic attack. My children were born prematurely and spent many days in neonatal intensive care even after I was discharged home from the hospital. This experience fed into the guilt and shame I experienced from the sexual abuse. I was convinced that my children were born early because God was punishing me for my relationship with Smite.

I also beat myself up because I could not keep my children safe and carry them to term, just like I couldn't keep myself safe

and stop the years of sexual abuse and rape. It was just one more way that I felt broken and damaged. I struggled some days to even get out of bed, much less be available for my children. By the grace of God, my mother and sister were able to step in and meet the needs of my children when I was not able to do so.

My inability at times to care for my children is directly related to symptoms of PTSD, in which I experienced overwhelming flashbacks or body memories.

For five years, I remember lying awake crying and pleading with God that if I died while sleeping He would not send me to hell. Smite had me convinced that what was happening between the two of us was my fault and that I provoked him into doing it. There were also times that Smite's touch felt good which created such confusion and shame for me. How could something that I know is wrong also physically feel so good? I am coming to learn that the physical pleasure was exactly how God created our bodies to respond to physical touch in relationships. The problem was this relationship with Smite was not a relationship ordained by God. God is still working on healing me spiritually as a result of my belief in that lie. Prior to about two years ago, the thought of praying, particularly with a pastor, deacon, or elder of the church, was out of the question. Just the mere thought of it would send me into a severe panic attack. Today, I can pray with a few of these individuals, who have been hand selected by those I have grown to love and trust.

Medical and Psychiatric Impact

The sexual abuse has also had an impact on my relationship with God.

Medically I have suffered as well. I have been diagnosed with fibromyalgia, an autoimmune disorder, and chronic fatigue from years of not being able to sleep due to nightmares and flashbacks. The fibromyalgia and autoimmune disorder are both common disorders for someone who has suffered from ongoing traumatic events.

I am in and out of the hospital on a regular basis causing a significant amount of time lost from work. Since I am in private practice, I take a financial hit as well during these times. When I don't work I don't get paid. Another way my family suffers.

From a psychiatric perspective, I have been diagnosed with Post Traumatic Stress Disorder and am on medications to aid with depression, anxiety, sleep, and flashbacks. I have spent countless numbers of hours and money in therapy to help address the trauma resulting from the sexual abuse and rape. The providers I go to do not take insurance so I pay out of pocket for

More than one medical doctor has stated, "You need to get this behind you because the stress of dealing with it is going to be the death of you."

these sessions. The amount spent on therapy alone is $1500.00 per month, which is one more way my family suffers financially. Even with the amount of time and money spent in therapy, I still struggle with dissociating from the present time and place when I begin to delve into the surface issues related to the rape and abuse.

The decision to pursue criminal charges against Smite was extremely stressful! Going to court created a great deal of emotional and physical distress on me. My autoimmune disorder gets triggered resulting in a great deal of physical pain and inflammation. The week leading up to and following a court date, I was bombarded with massive flashbacks and body memories causing the same cramps I had following the daily abuse by Smite those five years. It made it difficult to function on a day to day basis. During those times, I would find myself curled up in a ball, crying, and wishing I could just die.

> *I put myself through it because I wanted to bring closure. I wanted to find justice for myself.*

Shame and Depression

While all these areas are in the process of repair, I still have days where I look in the mirror and all I can see is a dirty, damaged, shameful person. I have moments and times where I hate myself and struggle to function because the depression is so great. I also have periods of time where I lay in bed and just cry because

I just want to die! More often than not I have wondered why Smite didn't just go ahead and kill me. At least in death I would not have to keep reliving the abuse and rapes over and over again in my head and in my body.

The sexual abuse endured at the hands of Smite will continue to plague me for the rest of my life. Smite was able to spend his life with his wife and family, not having to worry about the pain he had inflicted on me. His wife died believing I went after her husband! The truth is I never went after him. Any time he spends in jail is nothing in comparison to the life sentence he has inflicted on me and my family.

While my goal in pressing charges this late in life was not for him to do jail time, what I really wanted and needed was for a judge to declare him guilty. I needed to hear someone in a position of authority proclaim Smite's guilt, in order to be able to take the burden of shame and guilt off me and place it on him where it really belongs. It has been many years in coming!

Revealing the Abuse and Rape

Years ago, when my family reported this to the Christian school, the school avoided their responsibility to report these sexual offenses to law enforcement and Child Protective Services by stating that it was not necessary because, "Smite had an inappropriate, consensual, sexual relationship with a student" and was fired because of it. Smite has yet to be held accountable in any significant way for his actions by the Christian community, yet I live with the consequences of his behavior every single day. This journey, which I believed would end when I graduated from high school in June of 1987, has been a thirty plus year journey to healing.

While I am definitely better than I was, this journey is a lifelong process. There are definitely days that are better than others, however, there is never a day that goes by that I am not reminded of the sexual assaults and rapes encountered at the hands of Smite. That day in June of 1982, when Smite first touched me was the beginning of a life sentence from which I cannot seem to fully escape!

As I sought help for myself with a psychiatrist and a licensed clinical social worker, much was revealed about the process of healing from the sexual abuse and rape as a young girl.

Revelations from My Therapy Sessions

There was a point in one of my therapy sessions where I was really struggling. It was something that had been coming up over and over again in sessions with both my social worker and my psychiatrist. One of the things I finally became aware of was that there was another part of myself that was hijacking my system 98 percent of the time.

In the past we would refer to her as the fourteen-year-old part of me, but more specifically she is the fourteen-year-old part of me that was at my house the day Smite raped me. This particular part of me houses the sensations, images, feelings, and thoughts of that day. Yes, there were many other events that the fourteen-year-old part of me experienced, but for whatever reason this event at my house requires its own complete part. I guess it would be fair to say that there are probably two fourteen-year-old parts that need to be dealt with within me.

The trigger seemed to be when I was given an assignment to write out questions for Smite confronting him with what he did to me and the impact it has had on my life. As I began to go through that list at this therapy session, there were a few of them specifically referencing the rape at my house when I was fourteen.

All of a sudden, I found myself faced with the image of that fourteen-year-old me laying on the bed completely naked. The shame, the guilt, and the embarrassment started to flood me. I knew what was happening and I kept telling myself that I needed to tell the therapist about it, but I couldn't find the words. Instead, I just started to dissociate.

This is the fourteen-year-old part of me that shows up and highjacks my system because it is the part that houses more shame and embarrassment than I can even voice.

However, at that point I became aware that now someone was in my presence that could help me. There was a huge part of me that wanted to ask for help, but I just couldn't make it happen. I didn't feel threatened by this person. I actually remember thinking this person could help, but the shame and embarrassment and grief just became too much to handle.

The fact that I could not voice what was happening revealed that part of me definitely needed some attention and had a great deal to say. She definitely carried more of the pain, shame, and embarrassment than any of the other parts. Part of it was because she was violated in the place that should have been safe for her.

The other thing I learned early on in therapy was that when we did any kind of exercise where I was asked to close my eyes, my mind almost always went right to that same image. The result was a partial eclipse of my system. I would then find myself unable to open my eyes and look at whoever else was in the room with me. That was another indication of how wounded that fourteen-year-old part of me really was and how much she was impacting my ability to heal.

Questions for Smite

1. Do you remember the first time you kissed me and where we were?
2. I was only twelve years old. What on earth were you thinking?
3. Have you ever wished you could apologize to me for what you have done, and if so, what exactly you would have apologized for?
4. Why did you not give me and my parents a sincere, written, apology–something tangible I could hold onto to help me through the shame and guilt?

5. Have you ever wished you could ask me for forgiveness and if so what exactly would you ask me to forgive you for?

6. What damage do you think you did to me spiritually when you would teach about a loving, caring God one hour and the next hour you would fondle me or try to have sex with me?

7. Did you ever realize how humiliating it was for me to sit across from you at your desk or next to you, and attempt to focus on my work while you had your foot or hand up my dress fondling me?

8. Did you know how fearful I was that someone would see it or that my ninth and tenth grade peers would make fun of me because of it?

9. When you were touching my intimate areas, did you not realize as an adult Christian teacher that you were touching/bruising/wounding my future intimacy not only with men in my life, but with God Himself?

10. What exactly did you confess to the pastor that you had done to me?

11. What did you tell your wife about what you had done to me?

12. Did you really mean it when you would tell me that it was my fault that you were touching me?

13. Do you really believe that a young girl of twelve to sixteen could be responsible for an adult acting out on her in that manner?

14. If I told you that as a result of your actions I have contemplated suicide on several occasions and have definitely

over the course of several years engaged in self-destructive behavior, would you even care?

15. Why did you choose to molest and sexually assault me?

16. Did you really believe that I enjoyed what you were doing?

17. What words could you use to describe what you did to me in those years when I was only twelve to fourteen years old other than molestation and rape?

18. How can you claim to have a personal relationship with God or claim to be a "godly man" if you have this skeleton and this rotting corpse in your closet?

19. Do you remember the first time you forced me to have oral sex with you? I was only twelve years old. Did you ever think about how damaging that would be for a young girl of that age? Why would you do that?

20. Do you remember what you were wearing the day you forced me to have sex with you at my parents' house? You probably don't remember but I do. Every second of that encounter is engraved into my consciousness. Every smell, every taste, every bodily sensation!

21. When you raped me at my parent's house was it your intention from the beginning to rape me?

22. After leaving me that day, did you think about what you had done on your way home?

23. Why did you come back later that night with your wife? Did you know how scared I was to even see you after what had happened that afternoon?

As a side note, the experience of putting these thoughts on paper has been very challenging. It has taken me a great deal of time to work through some of this to even write about it. Just the mere thought of communicating how I felt while the abuse was happening and how it has impacted me, created a great deal of distress. It was only through my work with my therapists that I was able to do what little bit I did. At this point, it does not take much for me to be triggered and to lose sight of the here and now. I continue in weekly therapy twice a week: one session with a psychiatrist and the other with a Licensed Clinical Social Worker who specializes in trauma therapy.

➢ PTSD is very real for abuse and rape victims. If you are experiencing these symptoms, do not put off seeking professional help.

➢ A psychiatrist and a licensed clinical social worker who specializes in trauma therapy can be a great help in your journey toward healing.

➢ Find a spiritual mentor who can help pray with you as you seek to find spiritual healing.

➢ Keep a journal of conversations with God as you embark on the path of healing. When you enter those deep, dark, painful places in your soul, write about your bodily sensations, images, feelings, and thoughts. Then find someone you trust to share it with. A therapist for emotional healing and a spiritual mentor for spiritual healing. Both are important parts of trauma that require healing. You cannot experience healing in one arena without working on healing in both.

Chapter 3

Journey Toward Healing

In September of 1990, a girl in the youth group I had been working with told me that Smite was beginning to touch her on the shoulders in the classroom and was doing or saying things that made her feel uncomfortable. At that point I realized that I needed to say something because if Smite hurt her then I would feel guilty and responsible. When I came home for the weekend from college, I told my parents that Smite had sexually violated me. I didn't give them much detail, but enough for them to understand that he had molested me for almost five years.

My father went to the school and reported to the pastor that Smite had abused me. My father was later told that Smite's ordination papers had been taken away, that he had been fired, and was made to promise not to ever work or be around children again.

After I graduated from college, I came home to live. I started working more with the youth group. By the end of the summer, I was referred to a Christian counselor at the Minirth,

Meier, and Byrd clinic in Fairfax for counseling. I began counseling with him in September of 1991. I was in counseling with
him for several years.

In the Fall of 1991, I consulted with a law firm in reference to
pursuing a legal case against Smite and the Christian school and
church. At that time is was determined by the attorney and my
therapist that pursuing a case could potentially lead to me com-
mitting suicide. It was determined that pursuing a case against
Smite or the school would be too stressful and I was not emotionally healthy enough to pursue a case at that point.

In the Fall of 2001, I started seeing Dr. Charles for medication management and then shortly after for weekly therapy. In the
summer of 2008, Dr. Charles referred me to a trauma therapist.
Since then I have been seeing both on a weekly basis to move forward on my journey towards healing.

This Process Called Healing

As I continue on my journey towards healing, I am filled with
a great deal of apprehension about what I am about to encounter
as well as apprehension about how my life will be forever changed
through this process called healing. As I contemplate the healing
process, I begin to question myself as to what does healing
really mean.

Am I ever truly going to be healed? Is it even possible to be healed from the indelible marks of life's traumas and losses?

With these questions in mind, I set out to define for myself what "true healing" means in the context of my life. As I contemplate that, I have to look inward and figure out what needs to be healed. What are the parts of self that keep me from being a whole and complete person? That is where I would like to begin as I develop a working definition for healing.

To date, I have identified four wounded parts of self as well as four healthier parts of self. These parts of self are representations of the traumas and losses in my life, as well as the successes and celebrations that life has afforded me. When I considered this journey I call healing, I took inventory of the different parts of self and attempted to pair the wounded parts of self with the whole parts of self. The best way I have been able to do this to date is to go to those wounded and hurting parts of self and attempt to identify what their needs and desires are.

As I have gone looking for these parts, I have found they are in many ways connected. The state of mind or emotional tone at the moment will depend on what wounded state surfaces, thus determining which healthy part of self is needed. The best way to organize this process is to look at the different parts of the wounded self and to see which healthier part steps forward to engage with that wounded part.

Standing at the top of the hallway toward healing, I find that, to a large degree, the wounded adult is the part of self that is preparing to embark on this journey to healing. The wounded adult brings with her a great deal of fear and uncertainty, however, she works very hard at not letting others see that part of self. She does this by keeping everyone who comes across her path at a distance by utilizing sarcasm and humor. This protects her from the vulnerabilities of relationships and the probability of being hurt, while at the same time making people believe that she is letting them in to some degree.

As the wounded adult begins to slowly start to walk down the hall towards healing, she comes face to face with four parts of self that are standing guard outside an open door. She sees the light reflected in the room just over their shoulders, but finds them facing outward towards her. When she begins to inquire as to what is inside, she is met with a response from the Victim Advocate part of self that there is a sad and lonely little girl inside who is having a meeting with Jesus.

As her curiosity peaks, the healthier part of self begins to push by them to enter the room. Once inside she finds a seven-year-old girl in tattered and torn clothes sitting in the room, head in her hands, softly crying. Jesus is next to her gently wiping the tears from her eyes and enjoying just being present with her. As this scene unfolds before her eyes, the wounded adult begins to sense herself becoming irritated and angry. It is not long before the wounded adolescent appears on the scene. The angry adolescent brings with her a sense that she is the only one that can protect this little girl, but is also frustrated because she feels as if this little girl is continuously inviting trouble to which she, the angry adolescent, has to respond.

As the irritation and anger builds in the wounded adolescent, the maternal part of self, steps forward to try to comfort and console her. She is met with the adolescent lashing out and yelling at her, "Go away! You haven't been here before so don't come in now trying to help or pretend like you care." In astonishment, that maternal part of self feels her heart sink into the pit of her stomach and she turns to walk away, as the tears begin to stream down her face.

Almost simultaneously, the therapeutic part of self appears and gently yet firmly confronts the wounded adolescent. Somewhat caught off guard, the adolescent begins to fade gently into the background and I am face-to-face with and finally able to see the wounded four-year-old. Reluctantly, the therapeutic part of self approaches the young child and immediately can sense that her presence is threatening and frightening to the little girl.

The wounded four-year-old is the part of self that carries the very first memories of being sexually violated. She brings to the system that sense and belief that she has no voice. Regardless of what happens to and around her, her ability to remain safe is really more dependent on her ability to remain quiet and as still as possible. The problem is this tends to be the very thing that invites danger. Her sense of survival depends on her ability to remain as still and quiet as possible in order to not draw attention to self.

Once the therapeutic part of self realizes that she is creating fear and anxiety for this very young, vulnerable part she quietly nudges the maternal part to come in and provide comfort to this young child. As the maternal part approaches, the young child eagerly and quickly turns her attention to the maternal part of self, and finds herself melting into the warm embrace of a gentle and loving mother. Almost immediately you can see her anxiety and fear relieved as she begins to connect with the nurturing and love that only the maternal part of self can provide. For the first time in a very long time she is feeling protected and safe from anything that the world can throw at her.

Now that she is feeling safe and secure, the young four-year-old finds herself at the age of seven. Standing before her is this very angry adolescent part of self, expressing a great deal of anger and frustration with her. As a result, she feels very lonely and isolated as if she has isolated and turned away the only part of herself who she thought was her support. Noticing the confusion and loneliness of the little girl, the victim advocate steps up and begins to support and defend the little girl.

She explains to the angry adolescent that the attention the little girl is seeking is that of comfort and understanding. What she has been provided by the adolescent to date has been accusations and strong hatred. Upon hearing this, the little girl nods in agreement that she just wants to feel acknowledged, loved, and understood just as the victim advocate has indicated. While this is difficult for the angry adolescent to hear, she respects the feelings of the little girl and slowly but quietly disappears into the background leaving the little girl to come face to face with that adult wounded part of self.

This wounded fearful adult is not sure what to do next and does not know how to interpret the scene before her eyes. She finds her vision fixated more on Jesus then on the little girl, and begins to wonder what He is thinking of her as He gently and invitingly looks in her direction. Feeling a great deal of shame and embarrassment as eye contact is briefly made, she quickly looks away and is eager to turn and dash out of the room.

As she turns to dash out of the room, she is staring into the eyes of the woman of faith. This part of self provides the system with the hope and strength it needs to endure and persevere through any situation. Quietly, this part whispers to the wounded adult, "You are safe and Jesus is here to help and to heal." Somewhat reluctant, the wounded adult clings to the words of the woman of faith and quickly turns back around to engage in the warm and loving embrace of Jesus. It is at this time that she can feel confident that things will get better and that this is the beginning of her journey to healing and freedom.

Finally, the woman of faith and wounded adult leave the room hand in hand. Both are feeling confident that what lies ahead on this journey is tolerable as long as each part of self can recognize that the true healing is going to come when each part is able to embrace the love and comfort that comes only from God above.

Dealing with the Wounded Fourteen-Year-Old

The next step in my healing journey leads me face-to-face with the wounded fourteen-year-old self. As I take a step back and try to connect with this fourteen-year-old, I definitely feel nauseous and sick to my stomach. My head feels like it is spinning out of control and I just want to run far, far away and never look back! She is definitely feeling terrified of exposure and that people will find out her secret and will turn on her just like other people have. Her image of having the breath knocked out of her as she struggles to stay in an upright position makes me angry and critical. I want to push her away. I am trying not to do that this time, but I am finding it difficult to resist the temptation. My biggest hurdle is trying not to get caught up in what is to come, but trying to focus on the present. That fourteen-year-old part of self is obsessing over other people getting involved (praying with a stranger or worse yet being in a room with a group of men who will pray for me) which **screams** danger to this fourteen-year-old! She wants to run away and somehow cease to exist! Every ounce of my being is screaming to get her attention, but she is frantic and can't hear me.

Quietly, I just watch and wait for her to essentially exhaust herself yet not hurt herself. My typical reaction is to get pulled into her world of chaos and irrational thoughts and lash out at her. However, this time as I wait I find myself praying for God to give me the wisdom and the strength to remain present for this young, terrified, anxious girl and for Him to give me an open heart and compassionate spirit to not condemn, but to love and embrace her with the love only shown through Jesus. As I pray this prayer, I take some deep breathes and just wait. I find that my head seems to be spinning a little less and my heart begins to beat at a more normal rate of speed. My responses do not seem to be dictated by an out of control fourteen-year-old. I just wait.

Finally, she settles down and she just looks at me. As we make eye contact, I begin to feel bad for her. The terror that is in her eyes and on her face is that of a scared girl who so desperately wants someone to come to her side and take charge. She feels alone in a world where everything seems so much bigger than she is and she has to figure out how to survive on her own.

I begin to feel as if my world has just collided with her world. I become that fourteen year-old who feels so out of control that the only way I know to protect myself is to lash out and push people away with my words and my mannerisms. I feel as if no one seems to understand me or how I feel. Not my family. Not God. Not anyone. Most of the time I am not sure anyone even likes me. I don't even like me!

If she can contain the negative thoughts that talk her out of taking those risks, perhaps allowing herself to connect with people or individuals through whom God is working will help her to experience the grace of a loving God rather than just having the knowledge of that love and grace.

I try to talk to her and remind her that she is a child of God, made in His image, and not only does He love her but He also likes her. She so desperately wants to believe that and take it to heart, but dismisses it just as quickly as it comes. Why would she do that?

The problem is that her experience with intimacy is that it leads to violation, mistrust, and pain. How do I convince her that intimacy with God is worth taking the risk? She has had brief moments of feeling connected with individuals in the last couple of weeks and it was comforting yet scary.

Does God Like Me?

I realize that the fourteen-year-old part of self is very real and present. While I hate that she keeps appearing, it is becoming quite obvious that she is not going anywhere and that she is going to have to be paid attention to. That is a hard truth to have to admit. As I consider the sensations, images, feelings, and thoughts of this fourteen-year-old, there are different things that come to mind. I would have to say that she definitely feels tense, almost to the degree that she feels as if she is always ready for a physical altercation. Her stomach tends to be in knots or queasy the majority of the time, and she feels like her head is going to explode due to the pressure and intensity of the thoughts racing through her mind.

The images connected to this part of self are of someone who is always in a defensive stance and who is just waiting for the next attack. She is always on guard both physically and emotionally.

This fourteen-year-old has a difficult time with her feelings because they tend to contradict at every turn. While she wants to be noticed, she also is terrified of being noticed because attention tends to cause her a great deal of emotional and physical pain.

She is also very angry because she feels like she was created to be someone else's punching bag and sex toy. Others notice she is angry, they notice she has a "bad attitude" and they have no problem commenting on that. However, they never stop to find out why, almost as if they know the answer, but they don't want to ask!

In addition to the anger is the feeling of being terrified! She never knows what or who is going to be the next source of her pain or conflict. Her only avenue to deal with that terror is to lash out at everyone, even people who might possibly be safe. She just can't take that chance and be hurt again. What really angers her is when the people she lashes out at don't go away. Instead, they continue to pursue her as if she has value and worth.

Going inside the mind of this fourteen-year-old and looking at her thoughts can prove to be very challenging. All these things plus others are constantly running through her mind and the thoughts alone often keep her on edge and wanting to lash out!

Why won't anybody notice me?
Why won't people leave me alone?
Everyone is bad or will hurt me!
SOME PEOPLE ARE GOOD AND SAFE!

You can't trust anyone!
YOU CAN TRUST SOMEONE!

God doesn't care about you!
GOD LOVES AND CARES ABOUT YOU!

You are not able to keep yourself safe!
YOU ARE ABLE TO KEEP YOURSELF SAFE!

You are nothing but a slut!
YOU ARE MADE IN THE IMAGE OF GOD!

You must deserve this or it wouldn't happen?
YOU DON'T DESERVE THIS!

To complicate things, she is sometimes reminded or hears things that resonate with her and cause her to stop and think about where God really is in all this chaos and pain. Every time I am reminded of Luke 3:22, it causes this fourteen-year-old part of self to become enraged. The problem seems to be that we don't believe God likes us, but He does. That truth suddenly resonated with the fourteen-year-old part of self because she automatically thinks, of course God loves me. He loves everyone! However, love and like are two different things! It is His job to love us, but He doesn't have to like us.

Thinking about and paying attention to that thought has caused me to go back and rethink my assignment on how God is pleased with me. I have replaced the word pleased with the word like and it has changed the whole concept for me. So the question becomes, does God like me and what are the ways He shows this to me?

God shows He likes me by revealing Himself to me. God does not spend time hiding from me, but rather He pursues me (Psalm 22:24). He would not pursue me if He found me to be worthless and of no value. He is not going to waste His time making Himself known to someone He does not like or He perceives as having no value or worth in His kingdom.

God pursues me by using me as a tool through which He works to bring healing to others. He also shows that He likes me by being attentive to me and bringing people into my life through whom He speaks, sometimes telling me things that are easy to hear and at other times challenging me with truths that cause me to struggle. He also listens to my cries for help (Psalm 22:24) and He responds to them, sometimes by remaining silent, and other times drawing closer to me (Psalm 22:11-20).

While the thought that God finds the fourteen-year-old part likeable, that conflicts with all her thoughts and feelings that people are bad and are out to cause her pain, how does the fourteen-year-old part let down her guard enough to allow God to heal the pain? It is obvious God and those few individuals He has sent to her are not going to leave her alone.

Manifesting My Trust for Jesus

One of the ways my trust in Jesus manifests itself is that it gives me the hope I desperately need to keep going. It is the hope that one day this pain will be gone and I will be free from it forever! I would like to add this is really what this whole "healing process" that I am going through right now is all about. There are areas of my life that I think I do trust Him and other areas are still a work in progress.

I would like for my trust in Jesus to be manifested by my being able to give Him this painful part of my heart and not worry about how the healing comes – knowing that He has my best interest at heart. Not second guessing myself or how I think He is seeing me. I would like to trust that the people He has placed in my life to help on this path to healing are sincere and that they mean what they say. I would truly like to stop doubting Jesus and the tools He uses to provide healing. Whether I receive that message directly from Him or through someone else, I want to trust Him without resistance so I can take down the wall and turn all of myself over to Him.

I don't know what the whole process is, but I do know that I am somewhat resistant to some parts because I am fearful and probably a little paranoid that it will turn out really bad. It is definitely a work in progress.

I thank God every day that He has never given up on me. He continues to steadfastly pursue me!

As I continued on my journey towards healing, I contemplated the healing process and began to question myself as to what does healing really mean.

Am I ever truly going to be healed?
Is it even possible to be healed from the indelible
marks of life's traumas and losses?

With these questions in mind, I set out to define for myself what "true healing" means in the context of my life.

➢ *What are the parts of self that are keeping you from being a whole and complete person?*

➢ *What is your own personal working definition for healing?*

➢ *How are you going to go about getting to that place on your journey?*

➢ *Who are the individuals who are going to walk with you on this journey?*

Chapter 4

My Journey Toward Restoration

August 2012, I signed a retainer with legal counsel to pursue a civil case against Smite. The decision to pursue criminal charges was extremely stressful! Going to court and having this case continued created a great deal of emotional and physical distress for me. My autoimmune disorder was triggered resulting in a great deal of physical pain and inflammation. The week leading up to and following a court date bombarded me with massive flashbacks from the abuse. It was difficult to function on a day to day basis. Sometimes I found myself curled up in a ball crying. I put myself through this because I wanted to bring closure–I wanted to find justice–I wanted my children and clients know they have a voice.

As the day approached for my interview with the local authorities, I felt very detached and distant from myself. I felt like I was watching things happen around me but not to me. Life seemed to be moving, yet I felt like I was at a standstill just watching it happen! I realized that the fourteen- year-old part of self was very reactive at that point. In fact, she was feeling exposed, apprehensive, and angry because she feared people were going to judge her and see her as the horrible person that she feels she is. Almost overwhelming feelings of shame and guilt bombard her. Then the more mature adult part of self spoke to her telling her she was loved. Nothing that happened to her was her fault and that she was taken advantage of when she was vulnerable and she did not have the resources available at the time to cope with the advances being made towards her. She had nothing to be ashamed of or feel guilty about.

The Interview

On June 21, 2013, I walked into the local police station to report a case of childhood sexual abuse which had occurred thirty years earlier. Some would say it was long overdue while others would say to just forgive and forget. Regardless of what other people's thoughts or beliefs on the matter, I knew in my heart that God was prompting me to take this next step. God had been preparing me and so many others for this time and place. He had been paving my path with godly people who stood in the gap and encouraged and prayed with and for me when I found it difficult to put one foot in front of the other. This was and continues to be part of my journey toward restoration.

It was 8 A.M. on a clear sunny day in June as my husband and I sat quietly in the lobby of the local police department. I waited patiently for the special victim detective to arrive for our scheduled interview. I had thousands of ideas of how this interview was going to go—all based on the television dramas as depicted by Hollywood. My mind then shifted to my story. I began to have flashes of memory play out in my mind of the hundreds of time I was molested and raped between the ages of twelve and seventeen. My body began to tense up as my anxiety and fear began to heighten. I could feel my stomach tighten, my head started spinning, and I began to hope and pray that the earth would open up and swallow me.

What events do I share?
How much detail do I give?
Will he (the detective) believe me or will he think I am to blame?

These thoughts were suddenly interrupted by a door opening. Standing in front of me was a man in a clean, crisp, long sleeve shirt with the sleeves rolled up, a tie around his neck, and a gun holster with a gun around his waist. He seemed to be quite large, for the twelve-year-old part of self that was sitting before him, and he spoke with a firm yet gentle voice. He reached out his hand and introduced himself as he shook my hand. I then followed him through several secure doors to the third floor where there was a "victim" interview room. The "victim" interview room was not at all what I was expecting nor was it like what Hollywood depicts. I expected a cold uninviting room with a table in the center with chairs on each side. Instead, it was a warm, inviting room with a two seat sofa, a coffee table, and another chair. While the room was rather small it still felt safe and comforting.

Here I was sitting in this small room with the detective sitting directly across from me, every movement I made and every word I said was being recorded. To say I was feeling intimidated, anxious, and scared would be quite the understatement. I felt like a twelve-year-old little girl, who at that moment was wishing that I could feel my father's arms wrapped around me, protecting me from the rest of the world.

Over the next couple of hours, I was encouraged to be descriptive with my words in order to create a picture of what it was like at twelve to be molested and raped by her Christian school teacher. What it was like to hear the words and prayers he recited as he was raping her. Words such as, "This is how God loves his daughters. This is why God created you. You are beautiful and God says this is okay. If God didn't intend for this to happen He would not have made you so attractive."

As I recounted the events of the abuse, I was fairly certain that the thoughts and feelings of the abused twelve-year-old little girl, were being manifested in my account and testimony of those traumatic days. I was bombarded with the thoughts of, "Will he believe me? Will I get in trouble? This isn't going to end well for me. He will be mad. He will kill me. I am going to go to jail!" Obviously none were rational thoughts, but they were my thoughts. They were the exact same thoughts and threats that kept me quiet for so many years. They were the thoughts that had kept the pain and horror of those adolescent years trapped inside me. Like some kind of infection, those thoughts haunted me day in and day out and were slowly killing me.

Prior to this interview, I had reported the abuse to two pastors and my parents. The first time was one year after graduating from high school. I waited one year after graduating from high school because I had a sister one year behind me. One of the threats to keep me quiet was if I told anyone about the abuse then my sister would be next. I had to respond to letters he sent me at college in order not to let on that my thoughts toward him were anything but kind. I could not live with myself if I felt like I jeopardized the safety of my sister.

This particular pastor looked me in the eyes and asked, "What were you wearing that enticed this forty-seven-year-old man to do this to you?"

The second time I came forward was two years after high school. I told the youth minister and my parents what happened, hoping to get help for myself and other students who were sitting under the control and influence of this man. My father became so angry at what he had heard that he became sullen, quiet, and withdrawn. I got up the following morning only to find that my father was gone. He had left to confront this man who had hurt me. A man that he could not stand from the first time he met him. Unbeknownst to my mother or myself, he left the house with his shot gun in hand. My father ended up at my best friend's house where he talked to her father. This was a family whose home I grew up in and who were like a second set of parents to me.

After talking about what happened, my best friend's father called the school administrator, and the three met at the church office that day. It was finally out, people knew, action was being taken. This second pastor fired the alleged perpetrator and forbid other church and school leaders from speaking of this event with anyone else. At that time, I was not in a place to confront my perpetrator, which this pastor was asking for me to do. The church wanted to apply "church discipline." My father absolutely forbid any of them from having any conversation with me about this matter. At this point my emotional stamina, and the walls that I had put in place to deal with this abuse had begun to crumble. I was suicidal and pretty hopeless at this season of my life.

For years my family believed that the second pastor was sincere and sought to bring healing to my family and myself. It was only through the criminal investigation that this pastor's true beliefs and feelings were exposed. Not only did one pastor manipulate the situation to keep me quiet, but the other was deceptive in his response to the situation. This pastor dismissed this teacher from his position due to "an inappropriate, consensual, sexual relationship with a student." Did this pastor really believe that a twelve-year-old would consent to sex with a forty-seven year-old? It would appear that this pastor's interest was not in the well-being of the abused child, but rather on protecting the image of the church and school ministry. This attitude served to be as traumatic as the sexual and spiritual abuse suffered at the hands of the perpetrator.

Once I got to the end of recounting the events of the abuse to the detective, I braced myself to hear one more time that what had happened during that five years of my life was my fault. My anxiety began to increase and I found it difficult to make eye contact with the detective sitting across the room. My heart ached and I wanted to run and hide.

However, to my surprise the response I got was, "I believe you." The detective went on to share that he had been through the file provided by my attorneys. The files contained journal entries with written accounts of what had happened during those middle and high school years. Journal entries that I had not reviewed since the day I first wrote them. My testimony and journal entries stated the same facts and details. He was convinced that I was really abused and I was not making this up. The very thing I had waited thirty plus years to hear, I finally heard! There are no words to express the burden that was lifted as I heard the words, "I believe you"!

My heart leaped for joy while at the same time I crumbled into a ball of tears.

There was no suggestion that I provoked this man. There was no sense of urgency to shut me up and send me away. There was no judgement. Instead, there was someone in a position of authority who could help bring justice to a serious wrong committed against me. Someone who just acknowledged that I had been broken. That Shalom had been broken. An acknowledgment that helped unlock my soul to begin to hope again. It helped me to believe in the potential for restoration and to believe that there was hope from this terrible pain on this side of heaven. All through the speaking of three very simple yet profound words, "I believe you!"

The room grew quiet as the realization of what had just happened began to sink in. My mind began to be bombarded with thoughts. Then I found myself muttering out loud the words, "What happens now–anything?"

That question was met with an inquiry as to whether or not I had ever confronted the perpetrator. The answer to that question was a resounding, "no," even though the attorney had asked me to write out potential questions to ask in anticipation of a possible phone sting. That became the Segway right into our discussion of a phone sting. As the detective described the particulars about how that would happen, I became overwhelmed with emotion. While I had walked into that place hoping to be heard and validated, I was at a place now where I was being asked to do something to help move this case forward.

Telling my story and being believed by the detective did not end there. I immediately knew that not only did this detective believe me, but he was ready and willing to move forward in his investigation of what quite possibly could lead to a criminal prosecution. He became someone who was going to use the power and authority he had to try and bring some justice to my pain and heartache.

A criminal prosecution that seemed pointless to some who saw it as a thirty-two-year-old crime, yet to me it was a crime that was as real today as it was thirty-two years ago. A violation I could not escape from that had haunted me every day of my life since that June morning, thirty-two years earlier when this man crossed a line that was not his to cross. Sitting in front of me was someone willing to take action with me—not apart from me. I knew in my heart of hearts that I could no longer run.

After a forty-five minute break, and a role play with a female police officer, I was wired and the phone calling began. The detective called the last known published number for this individual, as I waited for someone to pick up the phone. After several failed attempts, a decision was made to leave a message for the individual, with a phone number, requesting that the perpetrator give me a call at his earliest convenience. If he returned the call, I would immediately call the detective and we would arrange a time to meet back at the station to return the call.

Once outside the building, my mind was flooded with the reality of what had just happened and the wonderment as to where this journey I was embarking on would take me.

God had brought me here and now I was being asked to muster up the emotional stamina and strength to finally confront this man—not alone but with the support, encouragement, and resources of other people who would engage this battle with me.

Am I doing the right thing?
Should I just let this go?
Is this what God is leading me to do?

Overshadowing my concerns, my husband's arms reached around me as he attempted to soothe and reassure me that I had done the right thing and that he was proud of me.

Smite's Confession

When we called Smite back and I told him who I was, he was very open and talkative. I told him I was trying to get closure to what had happened to me in middle/high school and was hoping he could help me. He was surprised I was still struggling because he said he thought we had closure a long time ago, but was happy to help anyway he could. He asked what he could do so I asked if he could apologize for having sex with me in high school. He said of course he was sorry for it, but that he knew I was still a virgin. I wasn't sure what that meant but just ignored it. I then asked if he could apologize for having sex with me at my house. To that he replied that we didn't have sex. He said the only thing he ever did was embrace, kiss, and touch me. He claimed he had no recollection of us having sexual intercourse or oral sex. However, when I asked the question again he stated it was possible we had sex and he just didn't remember because he was on medication that made him do things he didn't realize he was doing. He said if I said we had it then we must have because I am not the kind of person to make that up.

While the detective was thrilled because he got the confessions he needed, I was devastated. Throughout the rest of the conversation he stated that we had a consensual relationship and that I pursued him he did not pursue me. He also stated that we had a conversation after all this came to light and that we hugged and forgave each other in front of the church congregation. We never had such conversation!

He then went on to say how sorry he was and that God had forgiven him, he had forgiven me, and he asked that I forgive him and just move on. He also stated that his wife forgave me before she died for pursuing her husband and engaging him in a sexual relationship. At that point I became so angry I didn't know what to do. I just wanted to drop the phone and run! I felt so dirty, embarrassed, and ashamed. The detective was able to get me to refocus so we could finish the phone call, but it was difficult. I ended the conversation when he began asking me personal questions about my life now.

Once I hung the phone up, I started sobbing and had a difficult time pulling myself back together. The detective tried to reassure me that I did a great job and got Smite to admit to exactly what he needed him to admit to. He told me that Smite's accusations were just his way of being able to justify his behaviors in order to live with himself all these years. While logically I knew that, it was devastating to hear him blame me!

Three days later, after a face-to-face interview with Smite, the detective stated he had enough now to get a warrant for Smite's arrest and that would happen pretty quickly, but that the process of getting to trial could take up to a year and that I need to prepare to testify. I would also have to walk with the detective through the school and my house so that the police could take pictures of the physical location of where the abuse and rapes occurred.

I was about to enter into the next phase of my healing and restoration. It was only by the grace of God and the people He placed around me for support that I was able to continue on through the whole process.

God brought me to a place where I was being asked to muster up the emotional stamina and strength to finally confront this man—not alone but with the support, encouragement, and resources of other people who would engage this battle with me. He had been preparing me for such a time as this. Yes, I was frightened, but God was showing me once again that He was going to go through this with me. I was not facing the enemy alone!

> There was no judgement. Instead, there was someone in a position of authority who could help bring justice to a serious wrong committed against me. Someone who just acknowledged that I had been broken.

> Three very simply yet profound words helped unlock my soul to begin to hope again. It helped me to believe in the potential for restoration and to believe that there was hope from this terrible pain on this side of heaven.

> God sent me someone who said, "I believe you!"

> You are not facing your enemy alone either.

Chapter 5

God's Grace

God's Grace

The stranger in the mirror she sought to understand,
Wishing she could change her and love her as a friend.
Instead she saw a person who was filthy and unclean,
She hated her with a passion that never seemed to cease!

The rape, the pain she could not stop;
The guilt inside tore her apart.
She screamed, she cried, she stood aside,
She felt the pain intensify.

She laughed and smiled, she cried, and fought,
She was in a struggle but was never caught.
She cried for help but no one cared;
She looked around but no one was there!

People laughed and called her strong
They even said; "There was nothing wrong!"
They never stopped to look inside
And see the pain she had denied.

The rage inside was building up,
Her love for God she had given up.
Her desire to live had been replaced
With a desire to die to end her disgrace.

She questioned God's existence
She wondered if He cared.
She looked around for answers
But there seemed to be nothing there.'

She was just a child; who longed to know,
The freedom of just letting go.
The freedom of being free;
To experience life as it was meant to be.

She was just a child caught in a world of pain,
Her knees were weak, her faith was gone,
She found it hard to carry on.
Her life seemed good to those around.
But their blind love drove her in the ground.

God reached out with open arms
He gave her hope to carry on.
He broke her heart and helped her see,
that with His grace she could be free!

Karen Hobbs
1992

As I read through Psalms 22 my heart breaks! I feel as if someone has just punched me in the stomach. The question, "My God, my God, why have you forsaken me?" resonates with me. It feels as if I cry out to God and He doesn't respond. Daytime is consumed with requests to God to take the pain—night time with pleas to just allow me to get some rest. My eyes are heavy from sleeplessness yet sleep does not come. Instead, the loneliness and betrayal consumes most of my being. I watch and listen as people come and go throughout my life and tell their stories of God's faithfulness and love, yet I have to look hard to find it in my own.

Why did I have to suffer so much betrayal and violation
from people who say they love me?
Why do people look at me as an object to be used, abused,
and thrown away with no value or worth?
Why does it feel as if my faith is being tested and tried all the time?
How come these things happen if He loves me and I love Him?

Without an answer to these questions, the concept of "Jesus loves me" was just a concept in my life! Now I know that the pain and trauma I experienced has turned that concept into a relationship because most of my life has felt as if God was the only one available, even if He appeared to not be listening or present all the time. In this chapter I want to share how I discovered the amazing truth of God's grace and love even in the midst of pain and trauma.

Grace and Love

Prior to walking into a Maundy Thursday service, I prayed and asked that God would make Himself known not to just me, but to the fourteen-year-old that seemed to be struggling. God did make himself known at that service and continued through the night and into the next morning. God used the depiction of Jesus carrying the cross by Himself, and then someone coming along and taking up the cross to help Him to provide a visual for the fourteen-year-old to realize that she had to carry the burden and pain of her sufferings by herself, but God had now provided people in her life to help her carry that weight. She is not in it alone and she needed to quit fighting herself and the people God put in her life to help her.

Then as she watched the dramatization of Jesus being nailed to the cross, the fourteen year-old also experienced the nailing of feelings and lies to the cross in a very real and personal way. With each hit of the hammer to the nails, she could envision different portions of her pain and suffering being nailed to that cross.

There came a point when it seemed to be overwhelming to her as she began to experience the enormity of it all. Her pain and her suffering being just a thimble full in comparison to the pain and suffering that Jesus experienced on that cross many, many years ago. She was overwhelmed by the magnitude of God's love. It didn't make the pain less real or less painful, but it gave her a new perspective on the pain. It gave her a reason to work through the pain in order to fully and completely experience the magnitude of God's love for her!

In addition, I heard a minister on the radio say that sometimes pain and suffering is a good thing because it helps us to know the Great Physician. If it wasn't for my pain and suffering, I certainly would not be struggling to know and trust God at the level that I am being challenged to know and trust Him at right now. It is not comfortable nor is it easy, but the cross is the bridge between my pain and suffering to God's undeserved amazing grace and love!

Freedom Reigns

As I enter the large room, I am struck by how light and carefree the atmosphere appears to be. I am greeted by a couple of ladies who appear to be very personable, confident, and well adjusted. They welcome me to the home and apologize in advance for what I may or may not see or hear while visiting. They stated that I may hear from some very angry and unkind residents, but to just try and ignore them. The less attention they get – the better off everyone is.

As I stood in the foyer, I found it to be quite interesting. Looking around it seemed to be very open and carefree. I was quite amazed at how everything appeared to be so clean and put together. Looking beyond the foyer there seemed to be an unspoken mystery. I was not quite sure what I was sensing, but I knew there was something much more intriguing than what I was seeing from the outside. As I anticipated moving inward, I was a little fearful of what I might find, yet my curiosity would not let me turn back. Right off the foyer was a room that appeared to be a family room. Beyond that was what appeared to be a long hallway. I began to move until I found myself at the doorway of the living room. Most rooms I could stand in the entry way and see them in their entirety. This room, however, appeared to go forever. The more I strained to see what was inside the darker it seemed to get.

Reluctantly, I began to make my way through the outer perimeter of this room and embarked on a journey into what I soon would come to know as the inner chamber. The deeper I went into the inner chamber the darker and louder it got. The noise sounded as if people were arguing and yelling at each other. While it was hard to make out, I could see a group of people surrounding a table in the center of the room. My heart began to ache for the person at the center of all this hatred. Not one person seemed to be backing down from her. She seemed to be fading the louder they yelled.

Armed with a great deal of compassion, I ventured further into the chamber. I began to make out more clearly the table I first saw from the distance. I noticed that sitting at the table was a couple of people with their heads buried in their arms trying to shield themselves from the angry words being hurled at them. Surrounding them were several people who stood over them berating and insulting them with every breath they breathed.

As I continued to scan the room, I heard some muffled crying in a corner off to my right. I quietly make my way over to find four little girls curled up together, crying softly. My movements inside this chamber virtually went unnoticed by anyone except the little girls who were startled by my presence and appeared to become more distressed. I signaled to them it is going to be okay and backed off some as I do not want to create more fear in them. My distancing from them seemed to bring them some comfort as they fold back into one another as if forming a human cocoon.

As I stood there for what seemed to be an eternity, I heard footsteps softly and gently coming down the hall. The closer the steps got the more the darkness that surrounded me began to dissipate. As I turned towards the door by which I entered the inner chamber, there in the doorway stood a man with long brown hair and a flowing white gown. As he entered the room the darkness was completely eliminated. The darkness was overcome by the light radiating from this man.

A silence fell over the room as the other members of the room turned to look at the door. The people who had been standing over the individuals at the table slunk back against the wall as if trying to disappear. The ones with their heads buried in their hands looked up and almost instantly you could see relief coming across their faces. The children looked up and instantly jumped to their feet and ran to this man—leaping into his arms. He caught and embraced them with such love, compassion, and warmth. He did not appear to be irritated or caught off guard by their excitement. In fact, he looked as if there was no other place he would rather be then surrounded by the innocence and warmth of these young children.

Not really sure who this man was, I just stood at a distance waiting to see what happens next. What would his next move be? After a few minutes, he placed the children on the floor and wiped the tears from their faces and told them they were safe now. He assured them that he was not going to let anything happen to them. He then made his way toward the table. As he reached out his hand to greet the two sitting at the table, I then could see the scars on his out stretched hands.

Jesus had arrived. The individuals at the table reached out with some hesitation, not sure what to expect next. Was he there to berate them? Was this the end of their life as they knew it? Once they took his hand Jesus pulled them in close and he just held them tightly. He quietly whispered to them that he had come to bring them new life. They did not have to continue to live in the mire of shame and despair in which they had lived for so long.

He then turned to the individuals trying to disappear into the corner. They could no longer hide. He gently but firmly motioned them to come toward the table. He then thanked them for fighting so hard to protect these young ones, but also asked that they back off. Their continuing to shame and degrade the system was only hurting and not helping. It was now time to love them and embrace them each and every one for who they really are, children of God who are covered by His mercy and grace.

As the light permeated the room, a hall could be seen beyond the family room. As the residents who were gathered in the family room began to embrace and accept each other, there could be heard the sound of a loud moaning and inaudible cry from down the hall. As the residents became quiet and just watched, Jesus began His journey down the hall towards the pain and grief that echoed through the hall. Tears began to fill the eyes of the residents in the family room as the cries ripped through their hearts. This was a cry that was not unusual to them as they had heard it thousands of times. The loneliness and grief that echoed from this cry was almost unbearable for the human heart. It was pain that was full of abandonment, grief, despair, and hopelessness. It was a grief that could not withstand any comfort this side of heaven. Whenever anyone got close to this person, she became silent and withdrew within herself. She was so wounded from the constant abandonment and criticism of others that she withdrew at the presence of another person as naturally and easily as she breathed.

This time was no different. As Jesus approached, she found herself quickly retreating within herself and replying to His questions with a sense of irritability and sarcasm. Though she was working really hard to push Him away, He wouldn't go anywhere. Instead, He continued to pursue her. Once Jesus saw she was comfortable being in His presence, He gently but firmly invited her to look into His eyes. When she did she found a sense of peace and comfort that pierced to the depth of her soul. As He quietly sat without judgement, she found her guard come down and she fell into His arms sobbing. For the first time in a very long time she was feeling safe and comforted and cared for. There was no judgement, just love and acceptance and no hurry to move on.

As I stood and watched this interaction, I was amazed at how the simple presence of this one man turned what appeared to be a battle zone into a safe and loving atmosphere where freedom could perhaps follow. The same carefree and light atmosphere which I first felt when I entered the residence began to permeate into the inner chamber where pain and shame had reigned for a very long time. Perhaps this is the beginning of new hope and life for all who reside here.

Is God Pleased With Me?

Have you ever found yourself in a situation where you are asked to reflect on a concept or truth that seems to be foreign to you or seems as if it could not possibly be true? This is one of those moments for me. I struggle with this truth for numerous reasons, but the most dominant reason is because it just does not seem like a possibility that anyone, much less God, could find anything pleasing about me!

Luke 3:22 is a verse that I am frequently reminded of and every time I hear it I become angry, frustrated, irritated. "The Holy Spirit descended on him in bodily form like a dove. And a voice came from heaven: 'You are my Son, whom I love; with you I am well pleased.'" The context of this verse is that the Holy

Spirit descended on Jesus at His baptism, and the voice of God speaks this to Jesus. It is the physical baptism of Jesus but also the baptism of the Holy Spirit.

I more commonly hear a paraphrased version of this passage which goes like this, "You are my daughter, whom I love; with you I am well pleased!" The paraphrased version rips right through me to the core of my being and hurts! It is an odd feeling because it elicits feelings of pain but also of comfort. In my mind and in my heart I can't make sense of those two feelings so I choose to push them away.

Writing this book has challenged me to consider something different with this passage of scripture. It challenges me to not push away this truth, but to embrace it and identify how this truth makes sense in the world of chaos and pain that seems to surround me. The whole idea of God being pleased with me is a comforting one. The pain comes in when I consider all the ways God pursues me and the different ways that I choose to push Him away. I am not sure it has been a conscious choice up until now, but instead choices that are made as a result of reminding myself how much God must be angered with me.

That whole idea that God looks at me the same way I look at myself is ridiculous. The issue now is that by choosing to disregard the truth that God is pleased with me would be an active choice on my part to give into Satan and pull away from God instead of drawing nearer to Him, thus, I would actively be choosing to sin! While logically I know that God sees me as valuable and worth-while, I have a difficult time integrating what I know with what I feel. Perhaps it is not an issue of integrating the two, but rather an issue of no longer allowing my feelings to define who I am. While feelings are important and need to be paid attention to, they are not the reality of what is happening in the here and now.

Feelings are rooted in my experiences from the past, however, I oftentimes find myself relying on them to define the present. When these feelings are attached to traumatic events then my response to them leaves me feeling defeated and down.

The first thing I need to do is to acknowledge that God does love me and I am pleasing to Him. When the messages or feelings begin to bombard me to the contrary, I need to silence them and not give them the time or attention they are seeking.

Secondly, I need to continue seeking God's truths about me through scripture, prayer, and godly people. God is a loving Father, and like any loving parent He is not going to do anything to lead me astray. I need to believe He has no ulterior motives.

Third, I need to realize that God does pursue me out of a desire to know me and spend time with me, even though Satan would have me believe otherwise. I know as a mom, there is nothing I would rather do than spend time with my children. I long for that! God's love for me far out weights my ability to love even my children. His love is unfathomable. So His desire to spend time with me isn't even comparable to my desire to spend time with my children.

Finally, as a parent, nothing rips at my heart more than one of my children saying, "Mommy, you don't love me!" That breaks my heart to hear those words, even when I know they are using it to manipulate me into something they want. Perhaps God feels that same grief and heart break when I minimize or question His value and worth in me.

The reality is that this is a constant battle that Satan is using to keep me feeling defeated and down. While the battle is fierce most of the time, I need to recognize that it is Satan trying to take away my only stronghold—God's love! Without that I am worthless!

How is God pleased with me?

1. God is pleased with me because I am made in His Image.
2. God is pleased with me because I am His child.
3. God shows He is pleased with me by continuing to pursue me.
4. God shows He is pleased with me by continuing to speak to me.
5. God shows He is pleased with me by working through me to bring healing to others.
6. God shows He is pleased with me because even from my mother's womb He has been my God (Psalm 22:9-10).
7. God shows He is pleased with me by drawing near to me in time of trouble (Psalm 22:11).
8. God shows He is pleased with me by being my strength and coming to help when I am feeling defeated and down (Psalm 22:12-20).
9. God shows He is pleased with me because He has not turned His back on me (Psalm 22:24).

10. God shows He is pleased with me by not hiding His face from me and making Himself known to me (Psalm 22:24).

11. God shows He is pleased with me by listening to my cry for help. If He wasn't pleased with me than I couldn't go to Him. He wouldn't listen (Psalm 22:24).

12. God is pleased with me because I will bow down before Him and praise Him (Psalm 22:26).

13. God is pleased with me because I proclaim His righteousness (Psalm 22:31).

It is now time for you to begin to activate all that you have learned about God's grace and love in this chapter. It took me a long time to learn this truth. You have the benefit of reading about my journey and can learn from my mistakes. Go back through each of the ways listed above for how God is pleased with me. Read them out loud to yourself so you can hear what God is saying to you. After you have gone through the whole list, write a page in your journal about how this makes you feel and what has changed in your attitude about your trials and tribulations.

Then take the time to thank your loving heavenly Father for His great grace and love!

Chapter 6

Learning to Embrace Trials and Tribulations Joyfully

I have to go back and look at the words and/or convictions that I received after reading Dan Allender's book, *The Wounded Heart*. The book states that sin is the enemy of someone who has been sexually abused—the enemy is not the perpetrator. The sin being the inward determination to make my life work on my own, without letting God meet my deepest longings. When I first read that it angered me, but the more I considered it, the more I begin to make sense out of it and recognize that I do struggle with allowing God to fulfill my deepest longings. My struggle is not in not wanting those longings met because God knows I want to have those longings met. However, my struggle is allowing Him to do it without

What are the practical implications of spiritual joy, particularly in my situation?

having to have the assurance or guarantee that everything is going to be okay or that I am going to be safe!

First and foremost, I believe it is the recognition that "I have been sexually abused!" Not once, not twice but numerous times. Instead of believing that I chose to be sexually abused or that it just so happened that I was sexually abused! The reality being it was a choice by someone else. I had no choice nor is it what God desired for me or my life! The shame, anger, and bitterness that I harbor is the fruit of a sinful man, not the fruit of a loving and gracious Father in heaven.

The need to feel secure or safe before stepping out and doing what God is calling me to do robs me of the spiritual joy of trusting in a loving God who is my refuge and strength. It reinforces that faulty belief that somehow God was responsible for the abuse and that He won't keep me safe! The truth is God did keep me safe. He protected my heart and mind by not allowing me to be blinded to the truth of His love and grace, in spite of what Satan tried to do through the perpetrators.

Spiritual joy is the recognition that God created me with a desire for a close intimate relationship with Him and others and that it is not something I should be ashamed of. The double mind-edness comes in when instead of believing that God created me for those close intimate relationships, I punish myself when I have those desires or encounters by doing physical harm to myself.

Counting it all Joy

My brethren, count it all joy when you fall into various trials.
(James 1:2)

The book of James talks about counting it all joy when you fall into trials and tribulations.

How does one do that?
What exactly does it mean to count it all joy?
Is it speaking of physical trials, emotional trials,
and/or spiritual trials?

Reading through the first chapter of the book of James, it would seem that counting it all joy when trials and tribulations come would indicate that it is more of a spiritual joy. Joyful in knowing that everything that we encounter here on earth, whether it be a physical or emotional struggle, ultimately points back to recognizing that God is going to work all of it together for our good. While we may not understand or get why something is happening, we can rest assured that God is in complete control and that ultimately it will all work out according to His grace and glory.

The PHILLIPS Bible translation of James 1:2-8 says,

When all kinds of trials and temptations crowd
into your lives my brothers, don't resent them as
intruders, but welcome them as friends! Realize
that they come to test your faith and to produce in

you the quality of endurance. But let the process go on until that endurance is fully developed, and you will find you have become men of mature character with the right sort of independence. And if, in the process, any of you does not know how to meet any particular problem he has only to ask God—who gives generously to all men without making them feel foolish or guilty—and he may be quite sure that the necessary wisdom will be given him. But he must ask in sincere faith without secret doubts as to whether he really wants God's help or not. The man who trusts God, but with inward reservations, is like a wave of the sea, carried forward by the wind one moment and driven back the next. That sort of man cannot hope to receive anything from God, and the life of a man of divided loyalty will reveal instability at every turn.

Luke 15 begins with the Pharisees and scribes criticizing Jesus for eating and talking with the sinners. Jesus overheard them and shared with them three different but similar parables. The first parable is of a shepherd who loses one sheep out of 100, yet he leaves the 99 sheep in the open field and goes to bring the lost sheep home carrying him on his shoulders. His friends and neighbors rejoice with him.

The second parable is that of a woman who loses one of ten silver coins. She searches until she finds the lost coin and her friends and neighbors rejoice with her. Both parables are symbolic of the rejoicing that happens in heaven each time a child of God repents of their sins and returns to Jesus.

The third parable is that of the prodigal son returning home after squandering away his portion of his father's estate and living as a hired hand and starving for food. He went home and asked his father to make him like his hired hands so he could at least be fed. He asked to be accepted as a hired hand because he no longer felt worthy to be called his father's son. When he approached his home, his father was so happy to see him that he threw his arms around him, clothed him in the finest robe and had the fattest calf killed in celebration for the occasion. The older son heard the celebration going on inside and became angry. Anger and jealousy consumed the older brother because he felt slighted, even though he never sinned against his father, and his father never threw a party in celebration of him. The father explained that was because he was always with him and always had access to everything that belonged to the father. The youngest son who was lost is alive and found again.

The first parable is symbolic for how God searches for us. He is not content to just allow us to wander outside the fold, but will actively pursue us and bring us back if we allow ourselves to be found. The second parable is symbolic of a disciple's priority to find the lost. Disciples of God are extensions of God and are called to do God's work as well to seek the lost and to participate in the celebration of their return home or their being found.

The prodigal son is a lesson on humility, mercy, and restoration. The prodigal son had to humble himself in order to approach his father. The father had a choice to show mercy or turn away. God always chooses mercy! This chapter is indicative of a God who pursues sinners in order to restore them and give them new life. Even among criticism or judgment from others, God's main concern is restoration not condemnation!

So how does this apply to where I am in my healing process and my walk with God? As I ponder that question, there are lots of things that come to mind. First, the picture of the shepherd looking for his lost sheep is a vision of Jesus looking for and seeking me out in the midst of pain in order to carry me back to the fold where I can be loved, protected, and kept safe with Him. So many times I find myself seeking solace in the arms of Jesus the Great Shepherd. This is particularly important for the young wounded parts who have felt abandoned and forgotten, to know and sense Jesus pursuing them and caring for them. How liberating! Then to also realize that God's disciples pursue me, even the hurt and not so nice parts. God has sent people who can love and care for me, even though there are some very wounded, raw, and ugly parts. These are people who can see beyond that and can rejoice and celebrate with me as I find myself drawing closer to God and find healing and restoration in Him. Regardless of how much I push them away, they continue to show support and concern for me.

However, I think one of the biggest applications for me is to stop worrying about what others say. Going to the prayer altar every week is about my finding restoration and healing. It is not about what others say! To be able to humbly approach the throne of grace and recognize that it is in that place that God's attention is on me and it is about restoration and healing. It is the mere recognition that in spite of all the shameful things I have experienced, God's only concern in that place and moment is to restore me into a new and complete relationship with Him. What others say is not His concern! Hebrews 4:16 reminded me of this truth, "Therefore let us approach the throne of grace with boldness, so that we may receive mercy and find grace to help us at the proper time" (HCSB).

Another application is that which is found in the older son's inability to celebrate the restoration of his younger brother into fellowship with his father. The brother's response reminds me somewhat of the angry adolescent parts of self who lash out when the younger parts find peace, solace, and rest in the arms of Jesus and/or those who care for them. The adolescent's response is to be angry and jealous, however, the father acknowledges that part, yet still goes back to care for and celebrate the return of his son. That is the same attention that angry adolescent receives. We do not turn away from her. We acknowledge her presence and invite her to join in the process when she is ready – without judgment or condemnation.

The Gentle Stroke of the Shepherd's Hand

Every week, I have the opportunity to go to a place where I can get in touch with some very painful and wounded parts of self that hold memories of being sexually assaulted day in and day out for almost five years and encounter the Great Shepherd. In those few moments, I feel the firm yet gentle stroke of Jesus, the Great Shepherd. The place I go has a soft, cuddly lamb that I get to hold, caress, and stroke—very similar to what you would find a young child doing with a favorite stuffed animal or toy when they are seeking comfort. This helps provide comfort to a very young, hurting part of self.

This week, I latched onto that lamb, feeling like I was being ripped apart from the inside out. I took that soft, cuddly lamb into my arms and began stroking his cheek and looking into his eyes. As I did, the tears locked inside my soul began to flow. In that moment God spoke. In that moment I was a lost, terrified, hurting sheep and I found myself in the presence of my Great Shepherd. He softly but gently stroked my cheeks, wiping the tears as they fell, and even shed some tears of His own. He reminded me that He was holding me close and tight, and that while it felt like danger was lurking in every corner, I was safe in His strong, comforting arms.

When I find myself locked in the memories of the past and unable to find my way back to the here and now because the pain and turmoil is so great, my Great Shepherd finds me, takes me into His arms, and carries me, knowing that at that moment, I am not capable of finding my way back home by myself. What a true gift it is to feel and know my Shepherd's warm embrace in the midst of excruciating pain, and truly know that the journey which lies ahead, though filled with great challenges and pain, Jesus has me in the strong, yet gentle grip of His arms. It is in His arms that I can rest in safety and the knowledge that I am being protected from the wolves of this world, even if those wolves are dressed in sheep's clothing.

> *Heavenly Father,*
> *I bow before Your presence, perhaps for the first time in my life recognizing the value of my words and my prayers to You. They are not words that somehow when I speak they just fade into mid-air, but rather they are words that You take to heart, that You value, that You cherish – so much so that there are gold bowls that are full of incense which is representation of all the saints prayers. They are not only heard, but they are captured for eternity! What a humbling thought. You are worthy to receive all the honor and glory and praise –You redeemed me! That means that all my fears, all my anxieties, all my injustices have been captured by Your blood on the cross! They are no longer mine to carry for You paid the price for them long ago. You never forsook me or turned Your back on me, but rather You went before me – marking the path that would lead me back to You. Thank You, God for loving me enough to hear my prayers, as well as making a way for me through the dark and traumatic times in my life.*

Unlocking Memories of the Past

It is a sunny, brisk fall day and I find myself surrounded by the beauty of God's creation. I find myself strolling along a babbling brook with a mountain range on one side and field of wild flowers on the other. The mountains are splattered with beautiful red, yellow, and orange, and there is a faint breeze blowing through the tops of the trees. As I walk alongside the brook, I can feel the wind blow ever so gently across my face. I am enjoying the comfort of my peaceful place, tuning out those things in my life which distract me from the true comfort of God's creation.

Walking along the brook, I look ahead and see lying ahead of me a limp, lifeless body. From where I am, it looks like nothing short of some kind of animal carcass. As I move closer, I begin to see it is the body of a little girl. Her clothes are torn, tattered, and stained; air is slowly moving through her lungs. As I get within arm's reach of this precious little girl, I see her tear stained face and the scars consuming her body!

When she realizes how close I am she musters up enough energy to yell, "Stop, don't come any closer!"

When I try to explain to her that I am here to help, she tells me that no one can help her and that I need to just go away! My heart breaks as I see this little girl lying in this field. It is obvious that she has been beaten and battered and thrown away to fend for herself. The stains on her clothes are blood stains from injuries she has sustained on her journey down this path we call life! She refers to herself as being filthy and dirty and broken. She states she cannot trust me to help her because all anyone ever does is stomp on her and take advantage of her broken body!

If she keeps people at a distance than she stands a better chance of not sustaining any more bodily injuries, even though the loneliness and anguish she feels inside is tearing her apart! The tears inside begin to flow, but she works extremely hard to keep them from being visible to the outside eye, even though she looks at me with tear filled eyes and a tear stained face. She so desperately wants, and even needs me to reach out and touch her hand, but she is scared of being hurt, judged, and abandoned! Most of all she is scared that people will see what she sees for her life. A little girl weak from fatigue and scared that this is all that life will ever afford her. The constant barrage of flashbacks and memories of being violated and abused seek only to serve as a constant reminder to her of how unworthy she really is.

When I reach out to touch her shoulder, she cringes in pain. Physical and emotional pain radiate throughout her body. Physical pain because at this point in her life any touch has been painful touch. That is all she has ever known. It also hurts deep within her soul. There is an aching or longing there for relationship, but a realization that if she lets anyone get close then the only logical outcome will be more pain.

Suddenly, she begins to weep because while the touch is painful it also feels good to know that someone does care, someone does want to be with her, and that someone is pursuing her! She begins to question how unworthy she really is if someone wants to be near her and wants to see her for who she really is. Now she is conflicted. Does she remain in this place of bitter isolation only to protect herself from pain, or does she venture out of this place of isolation and experience the freedom that comes with being completely known by God and man?

As she sits and contemplates this question, she is caught off guard by the sound of wind rustling the leaves on the trees in the near distance. Suddenly, it occurs to me that this is the picture and voice that plays out in my mind anytime I am in a position of being vulnerable or exposed. This is the voice that screams out at me when I am about to be found out by someone and my secrets exposed. This is the voice and face of my own shame!

The revelation that this little girl is me hits me hard, but I know I must go back and help this wounded younger self move forward to healing and restoration. God has been working on my heart, mind, and emotions preparing me for this encounter.

"Hello, how are you? I am back like I promised I would be," I greet her.

"I am okay, I guess," she responds tentatively. "I was scared that you would come back, but also glad you kept your word."

"You have nothing to be afraid of. I am here to help you. I am not going to leave you by yourself to deal with all this stuff," I try to reassure her.

"How are you going to help me when you can't even keep your-self safe as an adult?" she asks.

"You are valuable and I care a great deal about you. I want to help you through this difficult time and to support and encourage you," I tell her. "I am not here to judge or ridicule. I love you and want you to be free from the pain you have kept locked deep within yourself for fear of what would happen if you shared it. Will you let me do that?"

"I guess," she replies, then quickly turns her back on me as tears begin to stream down her face and she quickly but quietly begins to walk away. Her soul is aching!

I pursue her and hold her as she begins to focus on the pain she is feeling deep in her heart. She is surprised at how intense and sharp the physical pain feels. Beginning her journey introspectively, she is blinded by the tears as she travels deep inside herself to locate the source of that pain. The darkness seems to be overbearing as she desperately attempts to maneuver her way through the halls. It is as though she is walking through the halls of a museum and on each side she passes snap shots of scenes taken from her own life. With each passing photo, she begins to feel more and more fear about the heartache she thinks she will find at the end of that passage way.

At the end of the passage way, she is confronted with images of her shame. She is looking in a mirror where looking back at her is a bruised and battered little girl with a tear stained face, and clothes that are tattered and torn. In addition to her own image, she sees the image of Jesus standing beside her with His hands extended toward her. She is surprised to see Jesus standing next to her much less reaching out to her.

Why would He want to be near such a broken and damaged person? What could He possibly want from her or with her? Doesn't He see what she sees? It is almost as if He is reading her mind, because He firmly, yet gently, invites her to move closer to Him. As she reluctantly and cautiously does so, He takes her hand and pulls her close as He embraces her and me. The two of us are now one, the wounded child and the adult self.

Jesus whispers in my ear that I am His daughter with whom He is well pleased. Tears began to flow down my cheeks as I begin to feel His love and warmth reaching deep into my heart. I stand amazed at the grace that is being extended towards me. Who am I to deserve such love and acceptance?

Gradually the darkness that surrounded me in the depths of my soul begins to subside as the light of God's grace begins to surround me. For the first time in a very long time, I am beginning to feel alive again.

Newness of Life

As I walk through a field of wild flowers, I am surrounded with a sense of peace and comfort. The bright pink, red, and yellow hues of the flowers remind me of the newness of life. The air is light and fresh and I take a deep breath just enjoying the beauty of the moment. As I continue to walk slowly through this field, my attention is captured by a bright light in the far distance. As I stop and look trying to figure out what it is, I become more and more intrigued. I find myself being pulled in the direction of this light as my curiosity begins to peak more and more.

As I get closer it becomes apparent that the bright light is surrounding a cross sitting on top of a hill. The light becomes dimmer and dimmer the closer I get so as not to blind me. The force to which I am being drawn to this cross is so strong that it feels like it is calling my name. When I get closer to where this cross is, I stand in amazement and awe at the beauty of the wood and the pain staking work that went into creating it.

Then, I see the slight movement of a man standing next to the cross, from whom the light is radiating. The light is just bright enough that I cannot make out who this person is or if it is even someone I know. I continue to approach the cross with some hesitation, but with a curiosity that could not be stifled. The warmth and love that is radiating from that direction serves as a magnetic field to draw me closer and closer.

As I get closer and closer to that cross, I begin to feel overwhelmed with anxiety and fear and I begin to take smaller and smaller steps as I am able to visualize the cross more and more clearly. Suddenly, I come to an abrupt stop as I begin to pay closer attention to the details of this cross that looks so beautiful from a distance. This cross has a story to tell and as I stand there looking at the various images carved into this cross, and the detail of each image, it hits me that this cross is telling my story. This is my cross! The man standing beside the cross begins to slowly walk towards me with His hand outstretched. As I look at His hand and see the scar on His wrist, I realize that this is Jesus waiting for me at my cross. My first thought is to turn and run, but something keeps my legs from moving.

As I stand there, I begin to feel faint and I find myself falling to the ground. Jesus swiftly, but gently comes to my side and puts

His arms around me. As I study each image on that cross, tears begin to stream down my face. Starting at the very top of the cross is the image of me at four years old clutching my baby doll tightly and wishing a parent would come in and hold me forever. The detail of this image is so strong that I can see the fear and pain etched into this little girl's face.

Continuing down the cross, there are images of me at seven years old on a gurney at the hospital, being rolled into the operating room, completely exposed to everyone who passes by. Images of a book room where the school abuse first began, images one after another of being sexually violated on a daily basis for five years of my life, a frightened yet angry adolescent who is bleeding and clothed in dirty, torn, bloody rags, and two preemie babies all alone in an isolette. Every painful and traumatic event that I had encountered in my life was carved into that cross and staring me in the face.

Overwhelmed with the magnitude of these images and the feelings they conjure up inside of me, all I could do was cry. I cried for the loss of innocence, protection, love, life, etc. These feelings were so powerful that I forgot Jesus was sitting beside me supporting and encouraging me silently. Finally, after what seems to be hours, Jesus speaks. The words He speaks are simple yet powerful.

He simply states, "Karen, it is finished!"

Baffled and somewhat caught off guard, I just turn to look at Him. Sensing my confusion, He goes on to state that the pain, ugliness, and condemnation reflected on this cross is just a precursor to what this cross represents.

"The cross that is before us right now is not the finished product," Jesus explains patiently. "The finished product is the hope that engulfs the pain and images on that cross because of My death. Therefore, it is finished! I conquered it all when I bowed my head and took my last breath. You are now free from this pain and ugliness if you are willing to leave it here on the cross and walk away from these images, yet hold onto the hope that engulfs these images."

Heavenly Father,

As I present myself before Your throne, I am struck with the wonder and awe of the mysteries that surround me. The beauty of the rainbow which surrounds Your throne is a reminder to me of the promise You made to Noah so many years ago. The grace You extended to him and his family to spare their lives and the promise to never destroy the earth again with water. The same grace that allows me to get close enough to see You, because without Your grace I would not be worthy to call You Father, much less be able to bow in Your presence. That same grace, which allows me to draw close and focus just on You as I set aside all my shame, disgrace, and sinfulness. I can boldly and confidently come before Your throne to bring worship and honor and glory to Your name, leaving the stain of the past behind. You are the God of all creation! My attention is also drawn to the slaughtered Lamb! He holds in His hands the scroll of which only He is worthy of opening! He is worthy because He redeemed me when He died and took upon Himself all my sin and shame and pain as His very own. The ugliness of my sin has been transformed by the redeeming blood of the Lamb forever and ever!

I bow before You, Lord feeling as if I have nothing to offer, but realizing that I have everything to offer! You see me through the blood of the Lamb and to You I am perfect and worthy of being found in Your presence. To have the privilege of being able to bow down at Your feet and to bring offerings and incense, which is nothing more than the prayer of Your saints is beyond any words I could mutter. I can't help but to think that some of the incense is tears I have cried many times because I did not have the words to express what my thoughts or feelings were. To think I didn't think You were listening! God give me a heart of worship. Take away the pain of shame and embarrassment and guilt and allow me to embrace the sacrifice of the Lamb so that I can boldly and confidently approach You on Your throne with honor and glory which You so deserve! Amen

Conclusion

My Spiritual Autobiography

Jesus answered and said to him, Verily, verily, I say unto thee, Except a man be born again, he cannot see the kingdom of God. (John 3:3 KJV)

How can a person be born again?
What does it mean to see the kingdom of God?

The following is my personal experience of being "born again" and how the events of my life are preparing me to see the kingdom of God with earnest expectation.

It was October of 1977 that my spiritual birth occurred. The events that transpired on that fall day were no different than those of previous days. I was physically born to Christian parents on November 24, 1969 and they were committed to training me spiritually from the beginning. They sacrificed to place all of their children in a Christian school and they made sure we were in church during our young childhood years. Their persistence paid off in my own life as at the age of seven, I asked Jesus into my heart.

I can remember sitting at my desk after a Bible lesson and my second grade teacher asking if anyone wanted to accept Christ. That October morning I raised my hand and she led me in the prayer of salvation. It was the moment that I became a child of God. I look back on that day and I thank God that He never gave up on me even when I had given up on Him.

I would love to tell you that I have been faithful serving God since my spiritual birth, but I cannot. As a seven-year-old, my life did not change significantly after my salvation. I loved God and I was excited to tell people I was a Christian. I knew if I died I would go to heaven.

My love and excitement for God changed, however, when I was in Junior and early High School. Having attended the same Christian school for years, I trusted my teachers and I admired their Christian stand and testimony. One teacher took advantage of that trust and he began to sexually abuse me. That experience made me begin asking, "Why would God let this happen if He loved me?"

I faced this man every day I went into class. He was teaching me what the steps of a good Christian involved one minute and the next minute he would be abusing me. I decided at this point that if this man was an example of what a Christian should be then I did not want any part of Christianity or the God that allowed this to happen.

My parents did not know the abuse was happening. The abuser threatened me and told me my parents would not love me or believe me if I told them what he was doing. He destroyed my trust in God, my parents, myself, and other people. As a result, I spent all of my High School years building a wall around me and pushing people away because I was afraid of being hurt. I also spent those years outwardly walking the steps of a Christian, but in my heart I was running away from God as fast as I could.

My High School years were marked with a longing to love and be loved by other people. I felt guilty for what was happening and was very ashamed. The abuse continued until the spring of my sophomore year. That same year my father suffered a heart attack which made me more convinced than ever that God did not care about me. It was at this point that I seriously began thinking suicide. I never attempted it because I was afraid of inflicting pain upon myself, and I did not want to hurt my family or the few friends I did have.

My junior year of High School started off really well. My best friend and her family moved back from overseas after being gone for four years, and the abuse finally stopped. I started including people in my life and began enjoying myself for the first time since the abuse began. About a month into the school year, it became very evident that the teacher who abused me had become very jealous of the relationship my friend and I had established. He watched as I became more self-confident and happy as a result of being able to trust in someone again, and in a matter of minutes, he robbed me of that happiness and self-confidence.

This teacher found me alone and raped me when I was fifteen years old. That day I felt humiliated as well as very guilty. These feelings of humiliation and guilt continue to be a part of my life to this day. The only way I have survived is by blocking the abuse and rape out of my mind.

I went on to graduate from High School in June of 1987. In September of 1987, my family dropped me off at a Christian campus in Ohio for my freshman year of college. From September of 1987 to December of 1988, I began to look to God to fill the loneliness that I had felt for so long. I figured running from God was not helping so I might as well try running back to Him. When I went running back to Him, He welcomed me with open arms.

Since that time I have developed a friendship with Jesus that I cherish with all my heart. I also began asking God what it was that I was supposed to learn from the abuse I had encountered as a young teenager.

In December of 1988, I transferred home to the community college. During the months to follow, I experienced the joy that comes in serving and trusting God. It was also during this time that I surrendered myself to serving God in full time ministry. I began to realize that during those early years of High School, God was preparing me to help other people. Because of the abuse I encountered, I became more empathetic towards people who are hurting and I understand what they are feeling. As a result, I prepared to go into full-time ministry as a Christian counselor.

God continued to work in my life and in August of 1989, I checked in for my junior year of college in Lynchburg, Virginia. The day of check-in, my family and I were in a head on collision that could have very easily resulted in death for everyone involved.

The driver of the other car had been driving under the influence and all he was charged with was reckless driving. My initial reaction was to ask, "Why, God?" The police officer told me it was a miracle no one was killed. I began to reflect back over the extent of the injuries and not only was no one killed, but we all walked away from the scene of the accident. That day God taught me how fragile life was and that every day I live is a gift from Him. I also learned not to take for granted my days here on earth because they can be taken away in just a matter of seconds. Each morning when I get up, I thank God for allowing me to have one more day to serve Him here on earth.

During the following summer, God allowed me the opportunity to work with the youth minster in my home church. I had asked God to do something great in and through me, but I was not prepared for what He had in mind. First of all, I had the tremendous opportunity to see the Holy Spirit work in the lives of the youth. I saw kids become excited about serving God and watched the excitement spread.

God also began opening doors in my own life. Ever since the abuse occurred, I had never really trusted people and never allowed myself to open up to anyone. All that changed one evening when the youth minister and I were talking. He asked me a question that caught me totally off guard. As a result, memories and flashbacks of my own abuse began to resurface. For the first time in years, I remembered things I had not remembered since the day they happened. It was obvious that God was using this youth minister to begin breaking down the wall I had built around me. I finally shared with him what happened and he became the first person I trusted enough to open up to since the abuse first occurred.

Finally, in September of 1990, I decided to tell my family what had happened. The evening I was to tell them, I was scared to death they would not believe me and that they would push me away. The youth minister agreed to be there as support when I told them, but before he came over he gave me two verses to focus on. The first one is found in John 16:33 where Jesus says, "In the world ye shall have tribulation; but be of good cheer, I have overcome the world."

The second verse was 1 John 4:4 which says, "Greater is he that is you than he that is in the world." As the night progressed, I learned that the fear I had of telling my parents about the rape and abuse was one of the misbeliefs Satan had planted in my mind to keep me quiet. My parents did not push me away, but rather they drew me to them and loved me. I found that the Spirit that dwells within me can overcome the fears and doubts that Satan plants in me. I also learned that God has given me a terrific family who loves me and cares for me.

Once I gained the support of my family, we were able to go to the school where the teacher continued to work and we became instrumental in getting him out of the classroom. Also, because he was an ordained minister he had to return his ordination papers and he is no longer able to perform ministerial duties. Through the reaction of my family and friends, I have seen where Satan planted misbelief of fear in my life to keep me silent all those years.

I no longer remain silent and as a result I am able to turn one of Satan's defeats into God's victory.

Growing up in church, I have found that many people believe that if a Christian is trusting God, spending time in prayer and Bible study, and busily involved in the ministry of the church, they will not suffer pain and hurt brought on by the sinfulness of the world. When I began to really hurt because of the sinfulness of an individual who abused and raped me, I began to question my commitment and faith in God. Since then, I have come to realize that my commitment as a Christian is not based on whether or not I hurt. The truth is as long as I am a human being living on this earth, I will experience the pain and heartache brought on as a result of man's sinfulness. Just because I am a Christian does not mean that I am exempt from pain and suffering. If God granted me freedom from pain here on earth, then I would not look forward to the day when He calls me to my heavenly home. My pain is what makes seeing the Kingdom of God so important to me. I know that one day I will go to my heavenly home where God will wipe away all my tears and there will be no more pain or sorrow (Revelation 21:4). I can have that assurance because on that October morning in 1977, I was born again.

If you have not prayed to ask Jesus Christ into your heart, you can do it right now or you can find someone who can pray with you. Your prayer can be as simple as the following:

God, I know I am a sinner and that Jesus Christ
died on the cross to take away the punishment for

my sins. I know that Jesus rose from the dead and is coming back again. Please forgive me of all my sins, and come into my heart to live. Please guide me to honor and follow You for the rest of my life. In Jesus' Name, Amen.

Facing My Abuser

For the first time in my life I do not care that I am feeling raw and vulnerable in the presence of other people. The court room is silent as people look on. My brain is being flooded with the comments of the witnesses as I was attacked by the defense and put on trial for a crime committed against me. The lack of empathy and the failure to take responsibility for the crime committed against me caused me to take these drastic steps in the first place. My faith was brought into question because I went outside the church and pursued legal proceedings.

"My malicious intent to seek revenge and to bring down this godly man and his ministry," was the accusations from the church.

"He is a man who is not capable of engaging in the behaviors to which he is accused and to which he plead guilty," came the testimony of another church member.

Listening to his son say that the only time he has known his father to lie was the day he plead guilty to forcible sodomy though he acknowledged that he read the transcript of the police interview in which his father gives detailed accounts of events I had yet to speak of to the police. It was a confession that led to five felony charges as it relates to sexual assault of a minor child.

Then I had to listen to the defense state this was an inappropriate, consensual, sexual relationship between a twelve-year-old student and a forty-nine-year old teacher. My stomach hurt, my head was spinning, and my heart was breaking! How is this possible when I am the victim here?

As I begin to regain my composure and the tears stopped flowing, I found myself praying to God that He will always give me the eyes to see when I have wronged someone and that I would be able to have remorse and seek forgiveness. As I finished my prayer, my attention turned to the individuals in that courtroom who truly believed they were God's disciples. It would appear they walked in darkness and were deceived by the world. I felt sadness for the people who sat in that courtroom who did not know God and who were being subjected to that mockery of justice. My prayer was that God would work in the hearts of all involved in the court process.

After the sentencing, I thanked all the key players and exited the courthouse by police escort. In the days and weeks that followed the sentencing, I have been met with a peace that passes all understanding. Sleep is more regular, flashbacks and nightmares are minimal, and I have a new attitude with the dawning of each and every new day.

I have been asked if I am upset that he only got five years. I honestly have to say that I was pleased with the sentencing. From the beginning my prayer was for God to work and be present. He definitely worked, and even with the defense making a mockery of Christianity and God, He still showed up.

How did God show up? He showed up in the words of the judge at the point of sentencing. The judge stated very clearly that he walked into that courtroom to give this man life. He went on to say that regardless of the sentence he gave – it would not take away what happened to the victim. Instead of life, he sentenced him to twenty years with fifteen years suspended, then serve ten years probation upon his release from prison. He would be a registered sex offender and would have to complete all the counseling recommended in his evaluation. The judge went on to state that he also was very much aware that five years just might be a life sentence for this now seventy-nine-year old man.

Do you see the grace that was extended to this man and his family? They certainly did not see it as they yelled out and cried out at the issuing of the sentence. The defendant became angry and resistant to the deputy escorting him out of the side door of the courtroom.

The family was so angry they remained in the courtroom while we were quickly removed and taken to a safe place within the courthouse. The police then escorted us to our cars as the convict's family congregated outside the door of the courthouse.

In the midst of it all, God showed up. God still offers His grace and mercy. How can I not be content with that? After all, He certainly has shown me grace and mercy even in the midst of my own arrogance and sin.

God answered my prayer that He be glorified through all of this. I am certainly more aware of His presence and movement in my life. It is an awareness I do not believe I would have gained if it had not been for this thirty-three-year journey. I honored the closing off of this chapter of my journey on November 23, 2014, when I entered the waters of baptism once again. It was an act and decision that was a demonstration of God's grace in my life and symbolized for me a "new beginning."

Now what? For thirty-three years I have worked towards closure for this earthly pain that is a result of this sinful world in which we live. I can't help but think that this place I am at right now is not unlike what the disciples felt when Jesus' time on earth was done and He ascended into heaven as recorded in Acts 1.

What now the disciples asked Jesus? Jesus said to wait and watch – God was still working!

I feel God is saying the same thing to me today. So what am I waiting and watching for? What does God want from me next?

I am currently in counseling and I am having to deal with the pain I have repressed all these years. The feelings I experience scare me to death and there are times I just want to give up, but God has provided me with people who love and care for me enough to help me through.

I can honestly tell you that I no longer blame God for the abuse and rape in my life. As a matter of fact, I consider it a great honor that God saw me strong enough to endure it. You see, that day I put my faith in God was not a guarantee that my life would be easy and free from pain. Faith in God means that

I'm going to look to God in spite of my circumstances. Satan attacked my faith, however, and tried to turn it into discouragement. Discouragement came when I looked to my circumstances. However, God's promise in 1 Corinthians 10:13 is that He will not allow me to be tempted beyond what I am able to handle, but will with the temptation also make a way of escape that I might be able to bear it. So as believers we are to accept trials as part of the process that burns away impurities, preparing us to meet Christ. Trials teach us patience (Romans 5:3) and help us to grow to be the kind of people God wants us to be. Trials, struggles, and persecution strengthen our faith and make us more useful to God.

Though I am faced with the uncertainty of what lies ahead of me in dealing with the painful memories and feelings of abuse, I know that God is here with me and that when all this is over I will be better equipped as a servant of Jesus Christ.

Appendix

Court Sentencing

The case came before the Court for sentencing of the defendant, who appeared in person with counsel, Frankie Coyner. The Attorney for the Commonwealth was present.

On November 17, 2014, the defendant was found guilty of the following:

FORCIBLE SODOMY

Presentence Report. The pre-sentence report was considered and is ordered filed as a part of the record in accordance with the provisions of Section 19.2-299 of the Code of Virginia.

Sentencing Guidelines. Pursuant to the provisions of Section 19.2-298.01 of the Code of Virginia, the Court has considered and reviewed the applicable discretionary sentencing guidelines and the guidelines worksheets . The sentencing guidelines, worksheets, and the written explanation of any departure from the guidelines are ordered filed as a part of the record.

Before pronouncing the sentence, the Court inquired if the defendant desired to make a statement and if the defendant desired to advance any reason why judgment should not be pronounced.

Sentencing. The Court sentenced the defendant to Incarceration with the Virginia Department of Corrections for the term of twenty (20) years .This sentence shall run consecutively to all other sentences .

March 12, 2015

Suspension Of All Or Part Of Sentence. The Court suspended fifteen (15) years of the sentence, upon the following conditions: Good Behavior. The defendant shall keep the peace and be of good behavior.

Supervised Probation. The defendant is placed on probation to commence today or upon release from incarceration for a period of ten years supervised probation, unless sooner released by the Court. The defendant shall comply with all the rules and requirements set by the Probation Officer and as shown on Form PPS 2 of the Virginia Department of Corrections, which are included herein by reference thereto.

Court Costs . It is further ordered as special condition of the defendant' s supervised probation that the defendant pay the court costs in accordance with a payment plan to be established by the Probation Office, which plan must result in any fines and/or court costs being fully paid during the probationary period .

Judgment For Court Costs. The Court orders the Clerk of this Court to docket a judgment against the defendant for the court costs.

Special Conditions Of Probation. The defendant shall fully comply with all the terms and provisions within the contract with the Adult Probation and Parole Department and including but not limited to all of the following:

If deemed appropriate by the Probation Officer, the defendant shall undergo a mental health evaluation, performed by the Prince William County Community Service Board or other approved treatment provider, and participate in any treatment required .

The defendant is to engage in comprehensive sex offender treatment evaluation and program facilitated by a certified sex-offender treatment provider and approved by the Probation Officer .

The defendant shall report to the Probation Office immediately upon release from incarceration.

March 12, 2015

DNA Analysis. The Court Orders that, prior to being released, the defendant shall submit to the taking of a blood sample for DNA analysis pursuant to Section 19.2-310 .2 of the 1950 Code of Virginia, as amended, et seq .

Sex Offender Registration. Within three (3) days from the date of sentencing, or within three (3) days of the defendant' s release from incarceration imposed, the defendant shall register with the Department of State Police and shall keep that registration current, all as provided in Section 9.1-903 of the Code of Virginia.

Compliance with this provision constitutes a special condition of any probation or suspended sentence.

Sex Offender Polygraph Tests. As a condition of probation, the defendant may be required to submit to polygraph tests as part of the sexual offender treatment program, at the discretion of the Probation Officer.

And the defendant is remanded to jail.

About the Author

K aren R. Hobbs, M.A., Licensed Professional Counselor (LPC). Karen has more than twenty years of experience working in the counseling field. Her greatest area of expertise is working with children who have experienced sexual trauma. She also enjoys helping adolescents and families through cognitive and family therapy. She helps her clients discover their individual potential while they endeavor to overcome self-defeating patterns of behavior that keep them from enjoying the life they were meant to live. She has worked in private practice and governmental agencies throughout the Northern Virginia Region.

Credentials

Karen received her Master's degree in Psychological Services/ Counseling from Marymount University, 1994 and through the State of Virginia as a Licensed Professional Counselor in 2001. Karen obtained her B.S. in Psychology, Counseling and Biblical studies from Liberty University™. renewingheartsfamilycounseling@gmail.com

CPSIA information can be obtained
at www.ICGtesting.com
Printed in the USA
BVHW04s0608260418
514429BV00001B/2/P